The Practice of Crowdsourcing

Synthesis Lectures on Information Concepts, Retrieval, and Services

Editor
Gary Marchionini, *University of North Carolina, Chapel Hill*

Synthesis Lectures on Information Concepts, Retrieval, and Services publishes short books on topics pertaining to information science and applications of technology to information discovery, production, distribution, and management. Potential topics include: data models, indexing theory and algorithms, classification, information architecture, information economics, privacy and identity, scholarly communication, bibliometrics and webometrics, personal information management, human information behavior, digital libraries, archives and preservation, cultural informatics, information retrieval evaluation, data fusion, relevance feedback, recommendation systems, question answering, natural language processing for retrieval, text summarization, multimedia retrieval, multilingual retrieval, and exploratory search.

The Practice of Crowdsourcing
Omar Alonso
2019

Predicting Information Retrieval Performance
Robert M. Losee
2018

Framing Privacy in Digital Collections with Ethical Decision Making
Virginia Dressler
2018

Mobile Search Behaviors: An In-depth Analysis Based on Contexts, APPs, and Devices
Dan Wu and Shaobo Liang
2018

Images in Social Media: Categorization and Organization of Images and Their Collections
Susanne Ørnager and Haakon Lund
2018

he Practice of Crowdsourcing

Omar Alonso

ISBN: 978-3-031-01190-0   paperback
ISBN: 978-3-031-02318-7   ebook
ISBN: 978-3-031-00225-0   hardcover

DOI 10.1007/978-3-031-02318-7

A Publication in the Springer series
SYNTHESIS LECTURES ON INFORMATION CONCEPTS, RETRIEVAL, AND SERVICES

Lecture #66
Series Editor: Gary Marchionini, *University of North Carolina, Chapel Hill*
Series ISSN
Print 1947-945X   Electronic 1947-9468

The Practice of Crowdsourcing

Omar Alonso

Microsoft

SYNTHESIS LECTURES ON INFORMATION CONCEPTS, RETRIEVAL, AND SERVICES #66

ABSTRACT

Many data-intensive applications that use machine learning or artificial intelligence techniques depend on humans providing the initial dataset, enabling algorithms to process the rest or for other humans to evaluate the performance of such algorithms. Not only can labeled data for training and evaluation be collected faster, cheaper, and easier than ever before, but we now see the emergence of hybrid human-machine software that combines computations performed by humans and machines in conjunction. There are, however, real-world practical issues with the adoption of human computation and crowdsourcing. Building systems and data processing pipelines that require crowd computing remains difficult. In this book, we present practical considerations for designing and implementing tasks that require the use of humans and machines in combination with the goal of producing high-quality labels.

KEYWORDS

human computation, crowdsourcing, crowd computing, labeling, ground truth, data pipelines, wetware programming, hybrid human-machine computation, human-in-the-loop

Contents

Preface

Many data-intensive applications that use machine learning or artificial intelligence techniques depend on humans providing the initial dataset, enabling algorithms to process the rest or for other humans to evaluate the performance of such algorithms. Researchers and engineers depend on human computation tasks implemented in crowdsourcing platforms like Amazon Mechanical Turk, Figure Eight, or internal ones as a scalable mechanism to produce labeled data sets. With these platforms, not only can labeled data for training and evaluation be collected faster, cheaper, and easier than ever before, but we now see the emergence of hybrid human-machine software that combines computations performed by humans and machines in conjunction.

To gather useful results, a successful crowdsourced task depends on many different elements: clear instructions, representative high-quality datasets, appropriate inter-rater agreement metrics, checks on work quality, channels for worker feedback, and good programming practice. Furthermore, designing and implementing tasks or experiments that produce thousands or millions of labels is different than conducting small-scale research investigations. With the explosion of new data sources like microblogging or social networks, labeling becomes even harder, yet more crucial than ever.

In this book, we present a perspective on human computation and crowdsourcing with an emphasis on practical problems and scalability. The topics and techniques described in these pages have a focus on designing and implementing tasks into a crowdsourcing platform and not in a specific crowdsourcing platform like Mechanical Turk or similar. That is, our goal is to describe methods that can be used independent of a specific platform or tool.

The topic of quality control, a fundamental aspect for ensuring good results, is presented from different angles as we develop tasks rather than restrict the content to an overview of certain algorithms.

We present examples of different data pipelines and applications that include crowdsourcing as a component for solving specific problems. We also highlight items that require attention when implementing large-scale systems.

Engineers and researchers can expect a solid foundation for applying crowdsourcing to their own research problems or practical tasks, including labeling datasets, evaluation, and survey-style studies. Our approach to crowdsourcing not only looks at designing work from the standpoint of results, but also explicitly acknowledges the human aspects of human computation.

The topic of human computation has evolved significantly in the last decade with a dedicated conference, HCOMP (www.humancomputation.com), and many tutorials and workshops in top conferences. This book does not attempt to provide a comprehensive state of the art of the many techniques and applications. Rather, the goal here is to identify the main concepts and techniques that practitioners should consider when asked to implement crowd-based tasks at scale. We assume basic familiarity with a crowdsourcing platform and some background in information retrieval or similar topics.

Designing and implementing good human intelligent tasks is a solid foundation for developing real-world systems that incorporate computations performed by humans and machines working together.

Omar Alonso
April 2019

Acknowledgments

The content of this book has grown out of material presented at events such as Data by the Bay, SIGIR Industry Day, and NTCIR, and institutions such as Microsoft, UC Berkeley, Università degli Studi di Milano-Bicocca, Universität Mannheim, and Max-Planck-Institut für Informatik. The author thanks the participants for their comments and suggestions which provided great feedback for writing the book.

The author is grateful to the following current and former Microsoft colleagues: Ittai Abraham, Tamar Bar, Dennis Fetterly, David Gerster, Vasileios Kandylas, Mark Manasse, Cathy Marshall, Marc Najork, Rajesh Patel, Alex Slivkins, Maria Stone, and Serge-Eric Tremblay, from whom he learned so much working on many internal projects. Cathy and Marc deserve a lot of credit for the numerous experiments and designs when working on social labeling and HIT debugging techniques.

Evangelos Kanoulas (University of Amsterdam) and Joel Ross (University of Washington) performed a detailed review and provided in-depth technical feedback that is highly appreciated. Thanks to Matt Lease (UT Austin) who worked with the author on a series of tutorials on the topic. Part of that content has been revised and updated for this book. Many thanks to Mateo Burtch who was kind enough to allow the author use his non-technical illustrations.

Finally, thanks to Gary Marchionini, Diane Cerra, and Sara Kreisman.

Omar Alonso
April 2019

CHAPTER 1

Introduction

> The story of organized scientific computation shares three themes with the history of labor and the history of factories: the division of labor, the idea of mass production, and the development of professional managers.
>
> David Alan Grier

We present introductory material that includes definitions, basic concepts, and mechanisms necessary to implement simple crowdsourcing tasks.

1.1 HUMAN COMPUTERS

It has been a decade of exciting work in crowdsourcing and human computation. What started as a cost-saving technique for collecting data has now found its place at the center of the new data-intensive world. Paradoxically, the more humans depend on computers, the more human input is needed for machines. After all, machine learning models need training data as input and performance evaluation also requires humans at some point. Computers are everywhere but there are certain tasks at which humans outperform machines.

Crowdsourcing is a term used to describe the act of outsourcing tasks, which are traditionally being performed by an employer or contractor, to a large group of people, often in exchange for micro-payments, social recognition, or entertainment value.

For example, say that we are interested in assessing the relevance of some documents for a given topic. We write a simple web form asking workers one or two questions, upload a sample of documents, pay for the work, and collect the results. Looks like a fast way to collect good results at a low cost, right? In principle, yes, but there are several implementation details that would make a task like this one to work or fail. Tasks are performed by humans not machines and, due to the nature of crowdsourcing platforms, the pool of workers may change on any given day varying the results and making the human aspect a pivotal role.

Existing crowdsourcing platforms make possible for developers or engineers to set up simple tasks and get results in a very short period of time in a fairly inexpensive way. However, the gathering of useful data requires not only technical capabilities, but also, and more importantly, sound experimental design. This is especially important in crowdsourcing where the interplay of the various motivations and incentives affects the quality of the collected data.

If we look at published research literature on crowdsourcing, there are three main beneficial properties of using the crowd for certain tasks: speed, cost, and quality. Tasks tend to go very fast, usually getting results within a few hours or less depending on the complexity of the required job at hand. The cost of running a task is usually cheap compared to a laboratory setting. We can pay a few cents per assignment and end up spending a small number of dollars in a single batch. Even if the task has deficiencies and needs further improvements, including the extra cost for debugging and testing, the final cost is still appealing. With the right aggregations, the output is usually of good quality. This does not mean that there is no need to deal with workers that are unreliable, but with some quality control mechanisms in place we can yield positive results. In contrast to traditional in-house editorial-based data collection methods that are usually slow and expensive, crowdsourcing is a valid alternative.

Many data science applications that use machine learning techniques depend on humans to prove the initial data set so algorithms can process the rest or evaluate the performance of such algorithms. Not only can labeled data for training sets and evaluation be collected faster, cheaper, and easier than ever before, but we now see the emergence of novel infrastructure and applications that combine computations performed by humans and machines in conjunction. Machine learning applications can only perform tasks as good as their input data and therefore much work is centered on defining high-quality standards for those annotations and construction of such training sets.

1.2   BASIC CONCEPTS

There is quite a bit of similar terminology accepted in academia and industry on the topic at hand. Terms like human computation, crowdsourcing, wisdom of the crowds, and collective intelligence are used interchangeably. We start by introducing vocabulary, definitions, and some, although incomplete, historical context.

In 2006, Jeff Howe published an article in *Wired* magazine called "The Rise of Crowdsourcing" in which he coined the term "crowdsourcing" and described a new phenomenon that consisted of outsourcing tasks to a large group of people instead of assigning such tasks to an in-house employee or contractor [103]. His follow-up book *Crowdsourcing: Why the Power of the Crowd is Driving the Future of Business*, took a deeper look into how the power of the many can be used to achieve what was traditionally done by experts [104].

A year earlier, James Surowiecki wrote a book that explores how large groups of people can perform better than a small elite. That is, under which circumstances, large groups of people are often smarter than the smartest people in them, even if not all the people within a group are especially well informed [231]. Related to the idea of wisdom of the crowds, collective intelligence focused on the decision-making ability of large groups. In both cases, a group of persons is needed to produce an output.

In the computer science field, von Ahn et al. [241] introduced CAPTCHA, an automated test that a human can pass but a machine cannot which has applications in security [238]. Many variations of the technique are currently used in practice for different domains. A few years earlier, the AltaVista search engine team devised a similar method to detect bots that were using the "Add-url" feature to boost pages or topics [161]. The subsequent work on reCAPTCHA demonstrated that the human effort required in solving an automated test can be channeled into a useful purpose instead of just wasted cycles.

Also in 2006, an article by Barr and Cabrera [21] appeared in *ACM Queue* describing a system that enabled developers to programmatically access and incorporate human intelligence into applications. The new system was called Amazon Mechanical Turk[1] and, since then, the website has remained one of the most popular crowdsourcing platforms. The creators of Mechanical Turk enumerated applications like audio transcription, language translation, image tagging, and marketing surveys.

While the work by Howe and Surowiecki looked at behavioral economics, the nature of work, workforce, and legal implications, computer scientists shared a common theme: data sets for training and evaluating machine learning and artificial intelligence problems.

The seminal paper by Snow et al. [225] showed how to collect labels for specific Natural Language Processing tasks using Amazon Mechanical Turk and started the adoption of crowdsourcing in many areas of computer science that have traditionally used editors or annotators for creating data sets. Similar research work followed in Information Retrieval [9], Computer Vision [226], and Machine Translation [40] that demonstrated the feasibility of this new approach.

The final milestone in our short trip to memory lane is the historical perspective on human computers from the late 18th century until the end of World War II by David Alan Grier [89]. In those years, a human computer was considered a job for doing calculations with nothing but pencil and paper.

In today's Internet world, the main idea behind human computation is to use humans as processors in a distributed system for performing tasks that machines cannot do well yet. Using the same terminology introduced by Law and von Ahn [151], we define *human computation* as a computation that is performed by a human and a *human computation system* as a system that organizes human efforts to carry out computation. The definition of human computation can be applied to any system that has explicit control over how computation is performed with a human in the loop, regardless of how many human computers are involved. That is, a human is executing a specific algorithm. Finally, we define *crowdsourcing* as a mechanism that a human computation system can use to distribute tasks via an open call.

Crowdsourcing platforms like Mechanical Turk and Figure Eight[2] (formerly Crowd-Flower[3]) are examples of online marketplaces for reaching an elastic on-demand workforce anywhere in the planet. Developers use APIs to submit tasks, approve completed tasks, and incorporate the answers into their software. To the program, the computation looks like a re-

---

[1]https://www.mturk.com/
[2]https://www.figure-eight.com/
[3]http://www.crowdflower.com

mote procedure call that is completed by a human. The application sends a request, and the crowdsourcing service returns the results. To the workers, they perform the task, usually in a web page or app scenario, and receive payment for their completed work.

The unit of work to be performed is usually called a Human Intelligence Task (HIT) or just task. The term HIT was introduced in Mechanical Turk and is also used by others. The individual or organization who has work to be performed is known as the *requester*. A person who wants to sign up to perform work is described in the system as a *worker*. When a worker decides to perform a particular HIT, the HIT is assigned to the worker. The requester can specify the desired number of assignments for a HIT.

We can think of human computation as an elastic distributed human workforce that is readily available for performing all sorts of tasks. While conceptually simple, implementing HITs correctly and automating the process requires a careful orchestration, as we will see in the rest of the book.

At the time of writing, the commercial infrastructure available for supporting human computation is still very rudimentary and imposes limitations on the kind of tasks that are possible to implement. Having said that, we are in the early stages and more promising tools and solutions are expected to emerge in the near future.

A viable alternative to the already mentioned platforms is to use the Games With A Purpose (GWAP) paradigm where users play a game and, at the same time, perform some labeling like in the cases of the ESP and Peekaboom games [237, 239]. The goal of a GWAP is to channel all the gaming interest and energy time to perform tasks that computers are not able to perform. If the game is novel and attractive, it should be possible to achieve high user engagement which translates to a large data set collected in a smaller amount of time. That said, game design is more complex and costly compared to simple HITs and could be harder to get proper traction with users. von Ahn and Dabbish present design principles for GWAP and describe interactive machine learning as an area where human computation can be at the core [240].

One of the first attempts to classify human computation was the classification system proposed by Quinn and Bederson [205], which consists of the following six factors: motivation, quality, aggregation, human skill, process order, and task-request cardinality. For each dimension the authors provide examples from existing literature, research prototypes, and industrial systems.

Wikipedia is incorrectly considered an example of human computation. Wikipedia is a free encyclopedia that is written collaboratively by volunteers and there is no algorithm implemented by the crowd. Thus, Wikipedians (Wikipedia editors) cannot be regarded as human computers performing a specific computation.

There are two items to highlight as they are common themes in most of the literature: (1) how to motivate people financially or by other mechanisms to perform a task and (2) how to control work quality. The first item is the biggest challenge with crowdsourcing: if we cannot find workers and motivate them to perform a task, we cannot incorporate human computation into new applications. The second item is based on the assumption that motivated people do not always produce good quality work so algorithms for enforcing work have to be devised.

Other facets of crowdsourcing like outsourcing work, open innovation, economic models, and value creation are outside the scope of this book.

"Snow. Snow is relevant."

1.3   EXAMPLES

We now describe a couple of tasks to show the basics of a HIT and what to expect when analyzing the results. Most of the HITs that can be found in practice are based on a simple form that presents instructions and data to a worker and collect answers.

1.3.1   QUERY CLASSIFICATION

Let us assume we are interested in building a web query classifier. To construct such a classifier, we need to gather an initial set of labels so we can train a machine learning model. We start with the following simple HIT where workers must categorize a given query according to a predefined number of categories. In case a better category exists, the worker can provide the answer in the input box as free form text. Categories are selected with radio buttons (), $QUERY$ is the variable that needs to be categorized, and [InputBox] a text field input. The template presented below has a title describing the task and instructions on what needs to be done.

```
Query classification

Please classify the following query according to the categories below.
If you think that the category is missing please enter your own in the
input box.

Say you enter the query $QUERY$ on a web search engine.

For you, the query is about:
```

```
() Music
() Actors/Actress/Celebrity
() Travel
() Products/technology
() Sports
() Politics
() I don't know
() Other [InputBox]
```

We run the HIT with two different data sets, D1 and D2. Data set D1 consists of 21 queries and 3 workers per assignment with an overall cost of $0.95, including Amazon costs. Data set D2 consists of 30 queries and 3 workers per assignment with an overall cost of $1.35, including Amazon costs.

Table 1.1 reports the number of workers in each data set along with the number of assignments performed by each worker. Tasks in crowdsourcing tend to follow a power-law structure. That is, a few workers perform most of the work. In practice, this can bias the results and one way to mitigate the problem is to restrict the amount of work that a worker can perform on a given HIT.

Let us look at some results for D1 and D2 presented in Tables 1.2 and 1.3, respectively. In both data sets, each query was labeled by three workers. Why the need to collect answers from multiple workers? We could use a single worker per query but humans are error prone and a simple error like clicking on the wrong radio button can produce incorrect results. Asking more than one worker helps us derive a more precise label.

President Obama and the Green Bay Packers football team are classified, as expected, under politics and sports, respectively (Table 1.2). In the case of Sheryl Crow and Christina Aguilera, there is no unanimity on the categories but redundancy provides the necessary assistance. If we take a majority vote, 2/3 votes, Sheryl Crow is classified under the music category and Christina Aguilera under celebrities. Using a single worker (say the first one), Christina Aguilera would have been classified as music.

What about if we run the task again with a different data set that contains some common queries also using three workers? Table 1.3 shows a sample of results for D2. Compared to the results in D1, the answer for President Obama is consistent but inconsistent for Sheryl Crow. The category for San Francisco is unanimous and if we use majority vote, Lady Gaga is classified under the music category. For the query Sheryl Crow, the crowd is possibly indicating that she belongs to two categories instead of a single one. The variation on the categories may also be an indication that our instructions are not very clear with respect to cases where a person is considered to be a musician and also a celebrity.

Table 1.1: Work distribution for data sets D1 and D2. We can observe that most of the work is performed by a few workers. In this particular example there is no worker overlap.

D1		D2	
Worker	# Assignments	Worker	# Assignments
W31	19	W25	22
W32	14	W33	16
W30	12	W7	15
W5	7	W3	13
W8	5	W23	11
W15	2	W28	8
W33	2	W16	4
W20	1	W36	1
W12	1		

Table 1.2: Sample of results from D1. Two queries have unanimous answers and the other two show variations.

Query	Worker #1	Worker #2	Worker #3
Sheryl Crow	Music	Celebrities	Music
Christina Aguilera	Music	Celebrities	Celebrities
Obama	Politics	Politics	Politics
Green Bay Packers	Sports	Sports	Sports

Table 1.3: Sample of results from D2. Two queries have unanimous answers and the other two show variations, one of which differs from the previous answer in D1.

Query	Worker #1	Worker #2	Worker #3
Sheryl Crow	Celebrities	Celebrities	Music
Lady Gaga	Celebrities	Music	Music
Obama	Politics	Politics	Politics
San Francisco	Travel	Travel	Travel

We finalize our analysis by reporting the number of queries labeled as "I don't know" or "Other" in Table 1.4 and presenting a few examples of category names provided by workers in Table 1.5.

Table 1.4: Percentage of queries that were labeled as "I don't know" or "Other" by at least one worker

Data Set	I Don't Know	Other
D1	5%	29%
D2	17%	50%

Table 1.5: Sample of queries where at least one worker provided an alternative category

Data Set	Query	Worker #1	Worker #2	Worker #3
D1	Jesse James	Celebrities	Gang leader	Robbery
D1	Twitter	Technology	Social network	Technology
D2	Wall Street	Economy	Financial market	Business
D2	Attribute grammars	Technology	Education	Formal Grammar

1.3.2   FLIP A COIN

Our second example is different. Here the goal is to replicate the experiment of tossing a fair coin and analyze the results to see if the output resemble the expected distribution. The template presented below shows the HIT with the basic request. We run the HIT twice producing two data sets, D1 and D2. The payment for each assignment is $0.05 with the total cost of $7 per run. One hundred workers were asked in each run.

```
Flip a coin

Please flip a coin and report if you got a tail or head.

This is a very simple experiment so please be honest with your answers:
flip a real coin and report the result.
If you don't have a coin, please do not work on this experiment.

1- Which coin was used?
```

```
() U.S. Dollar (e.g., dollar, quarter, dime, nickel)
() Euro (e.g., cents, 1 euro, 2 euro)
() Other. Please specify: [InputBox]

2- What did you get as a result?

() Head
() Tail
```

How did workers perform in our experiments? By looking at the results for question 2 in Table 1.6, we are closer to a 40–60% distribution which is different from what we were expecting. Running the HIT twice is not a guarantee that we can improve on the outcome.

Table 1.6: Results for the coin toss question for data sets D1 and D2

D1		D2	
Question 1	Frequency	Question 1	Frequency
Head	57	Head	55
Tail	43	Head	45

The law of large numbers states that the larger the sample, the less variability in the sample proportions. Would increasing the number of workers improve the results? Did head get more selections than tail because it was the first choice? Did the order of questions influence the results?

In this HIT, we included a specific question on the type of coin that was used (Table 1.7) as quality control and in several cases the workers explicitly provided the details of the type of coin (Table 1.8). Were workers honest in reporting the coin type? In D1, the coin distribution resembles the demographics of Mechanical Turk but D2 shows different demographics.

Table 1.7: Coin-type frequency distribution shows predominant U.S. currency

D1		D2	
Question 1	Frequency	Question 1	Frequency
U.S. dollar	56	U.S. dollar	89
Euro	11	Euro	4
Other	30	Other	7
No answer	3	No answer	0

Table 1.8: Aggregated results by currency

D1		D2	
Currency	Frequency	Currency	Frequency
Dollar	56	Dollar	89
Indian Rupee	20	Euro	4
Euro	11	Indian Rupee	2
Canadian	5	Canadian	2
Unspecified	3	Pound Sterling	2
Colombian peso	1	Brazil Real	1
Jamaican	1		
Dinar	1		
Serbian Dinar	1		
Ukraine	1		

1.4   SOME GENERIC OBSERVATIONS

Looking at both HIT examples and results in more detail, there are some observations that need to be made.

- Instructions are very important. In the query classification example, we have seen queries that are classified as music and celebrity by different workers. The instructions that we provided are not very clear with respect to ambiguous cases and there are no examples that a worker can use, thus we cannot blame a worker if a query was not classified as we expected. Furthermore, we use a very confusing category name in the case of `Actors/Actress/Celebrity` that conflates many labels. Before running the task again, we need to improve the instructions.

- Different runs will produce variations on the results. Due to the nature of crowdsourcing platforms, the pool of workers may vary on any given day. Statistically, this should not be a surprise as errors and variations are expected when running many experiments. In contrast to measurements provided by different machines where errors tend to be small, human-provided labels may amplify the variations. In terms of sampling and population, statistical analysis tell us that (1) sample results vary by chance and (2) the pattern of chance variation depends on the population.

- Aggregations can be significant. Humans are error prone and it is usually good practice to ask more than one worker and collect judgments for computing aggregation functions. Relying on a single worker may produce incorrect results.

- Agreements and disagreements are useful signals. The case for agreement is obvious: we expect high-quality results and measuring agreement is one way to estimate the consistency of the results. We should not discard a data set just because workers did not agree. Disagreements can shed light into potential issues on the task design or much bigger problems like task difficulty.

- Trust and work quality matter. We trust workers provide an honest answer. In the web query classification example, the results are what we expected. The task is simple and with some basic rules we can derive quality results. In the case of flip a coin, we trust the worker has access to a coin but we do not really know. Sometimes, workers have good intentions but the answers they provide are not good. Most of the current research on quality control uses an adversarial approach. That is, identification of bad workers that are gaming the system to earn money without performing good work. While the presence of spammers is a reality in any system that involves a monetary incentive, the assumption that a task design has no defects is unrealistic.

- Free-form open-ended questions are necessary. The extra feedback as a potential signal is very appealing. However, as with any data entry mechanism, data will be noisy and it requires cleaning before it can be used. In the web query classification example, there is value on the extra categories provided by workers (e.g., economy, financial market, business) but such data need to be grouped together. Similarly, in the flip a coin example, workers provided similar names to the coin currency (e.g., Indian Rupee, INR, rupee coin).

- Worker population is a factor. By looking at the answers in the second example for our open-ended question, we observe an initial distribution of countries. As we will see later in other chapters, there are ways to obtain demographic information from workers. HITs, therefore, must be designed in such a way that anybody can understand instructions and can perform work.

1.5   A NOTE ON PLATFORMS

Most of the published research on crowdsourcing-based experimentation is based on the Amazon Mechanical Turk platform with very little reporting of other platforms. However, while Mechanical Turk has influenced tremendously research and practice, crowdsourcing is not a synonym for Mechanical Turk and using a single platform for research and experimentation has implications for research questions, methodologies, and future directions.

Competition in this area is growing rapidly and there are a number of emerging companies that provide similar functionality or implement wrappers around Mechanical Turk. Feature comparison among different services is out of the scope for this book. However, these services are all fairly similar at the conceptual level. Vakharia and Lease performed a qualitative content analysis on seven crowdsourcing platforms: ClickWorker, CloudFactory, CrowdFlower,

WorkFusion, CrowdSource, LeadGenius, and oDesk [235]. The authors provide a criteria for assessing platforms that enables comparisons among different platforms.

Peer et al. [203] examine CrowdFlower and Prolific Academic and suggest that both platforms show adequate data quality and can be a viable alternative to Mechanical Turk. In this investigation, however, Prolific Academic was slower for collecting answers.

We assume that current commercial crowdsourcing platforms have limited tools and, in practice, we have to work around these limitations. This is, at some level, expected because the area is new and we expect better functionality in the near future. Like with any emerging technology, developers have to build components to leverage work on demand in the best way possible. If an ad-hoc process is used, the implementation could be expensive and very difficult to maintain in the long run.

1.6   THE IMPORTANCE OF LABELS

Assigning a label is usually considered a judgment task, performed by a human (e.g., worker, expert, judge, annotator, rater, etc.) where the judgments may be more or less subjective. Researchers and practitioners in information retrieval, machine learning, recommender systems, machine translation, and natural language processing use crowdsourcing techniques as a good alternative for collecting labels in a cost-effective way with comparable quality.

Let us examine the lifecycle of a label or, in other words, the flow and utility of a label in the context of a search engine machinery. In information retrieval applications, like a search engine, the relevance assessment process consists of showing a query-document pair to a worker along with a question ("Is this document relevant?") and some possible answers ("Very relevant, Somewhat relevant, Not relevant").

A human, with his/her own specific characteristics (e.g., expertise, world-knowledge and bias), judges a specific document according to a topic or query and provides a judgment. Because humans can be inaccurate, a common strategy is to use redundancy, that is, ask one or more humans to judge the same document and, in aggregate, produce a final label. Assessing a large collection of documents like the Web is not practical and an automated strategy is needed. That label provided by humans is used to train a machine learning model that can predict the labels for the rest of the document collection. Finally, the performance of the predictive model is evaluated with the label. As we can see in Figure 1.1, those labels are used in many parts of the processing pipeline and it is important that their quality is high otherwise it can have severe impact on the outcome. Like the old saying: garbage in, garbage out. The point is clear: good labels are a precondition for automatically processing the rest of a data set with equal quality. While intuitively obvious, labeling in practice tends to be rushed and not performed in a principled way.

In this new data-driven world, good labels are of fundamental importance for a wide range of applications. Developers and data engineers designing and implementing data pipelines that include human computation face new challenges. To gather reliable labels and produce useful

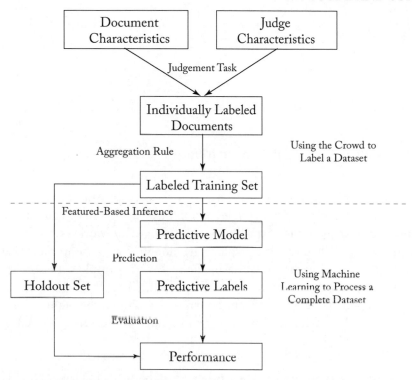

Figure 1.1: The cascading effect of labels in the context of document assessment for information retrieval. Using crowdsourcing to label an initial data set that later is used to process the entire data set using machine learning.

results, a successful labeling task relies on many different elements: from clear instructions to algorithms for work quality control. Constructing software for tasks that produce and use several thousands or millions of labels is very different than running small-scale research investigations. This may look daunting at first, but as we will see later, there are good techniques that can help us achieve our goal. Our approach to implement crowd-based applications is similar to software development, with a focus on both design and operational issues.

1.7   SCOPE AND STRUCTURE

We do not claim to provide a comprehensive account of all existing works on human computation and crowdsourcing; rather, we describe the many facets of this new and exciting topic that researchers and practitioners need to be aware of. The goal of the book is to lay down the fundamentals that are needed when incorporating human computation as part of system development.

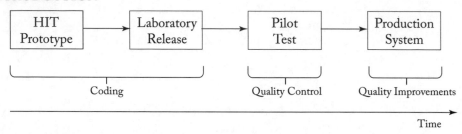

Figure 1.2: Methodology for designing and implementing HITs.

The structure of this book follows the incremental development process presented in Figure 1.2. The next chapter covers different angles of microtask design so we can start coding HITs. Chapters 3 and 4 look at the topic of quality by examining data, workers, work, HITs, and algorithms. The purpose of Chapter 5 is to explore the human side of the workers that participate in crowdsourcing tasks, an important aspect in the real world. Implementation guidelines for developing microtasks at scale are introduced in Chapter 6. Chapter 7 describes examples of existing data pipelines and systems in different domains that showcase combinations of different techniques. We conclude in Chapter 8 with current research directions and open problems.

Pointers

For people interested in this area there are other great books ([151], [171], [61], [87]) and tutorials ([236], [111], [155]) that cover topics that are omitted in this work. Doan et al. [67] provide a taxonomy of crowdsourcing systems on the Web and outline design challenges for new systems.

CHAPTER 2

Designing and Developing Microtasks

Machines have no common sense; they do exactly as they are told, no more and no less.

Donald Knuth

Errare humanum est.

Seneca

In this chapter, we focus on implementing crowdsourced tasks, HIT design decisions, and present examples from our own experiences.

2.1 MICROTASK DEVELOPMENT FLOW

A microtask is the simplest task that can be performed by a worker in a crowdsourcing platform. We should think of a microtask as a self-contained HIT that presents clear instructions that, when followed correctly by a worker, collects the labels required by the requester. We can characterize the flow of microtask development and execution as follows.

1. Define and scope the task. For example, document relevance assessment, image tagging, or query classification.

2. Design and implement a HIT for a task. A simple design would likely consists of a form that presents an object and asks one question. In the case of relevance assessment, the object can be a query-document pair along with some instructions depending on if the task is a binary or graded relevance assessment.

3. Assign runtime information. Before we can launch our HIT, we need to define the number of workers that are needed and how much are we paying for work including bonus and incentives. Other important metadata, like task description, keywords, and worker qualifications, are needed so workers can find our task in the system.

4. Execute the task in production. Prepare a data set for the HIT and launch it in the real world so workers can perform our task. In most cases, we will execute our HIT many times

with different data sets and, like in software engineering, bugs may surface that need to be fixed before labeling a new data set.

5. Collect and analyze the results. Once the HIT has been completed, the final step is to look at the work provided by the workers and compute results.

Given, at a high level, the similarities with running and executing experiments, the already mentioned list looks straightforward and easy, right? Unfortunately, things in practice tend to get more complicated as we will see in the rest of the book.

2.2   PROGRAMMING HITS

We are going to look at the design and implementation of a HIT in the same way we do with any software artifact. That is, using well-known programming techniques and other principles for writing short and manageable HITs that are easy to understand (by workers and requesters) and that work well in a number of situations. In other words, a HIT is like any other piece of code.

Similar to software design, there is no recipe to produce good HIT designs. We follow the same philosophy described by Ousterhout [194] and try to enumerate red flags or common problems instead of a specific procedure. Like in computer programming, the goal is to minimize complexity, think in terms of problem de-composition, and, above everything, get lots of practice.

We should always try to design and program HITs into a crowdsourcing platform and not in a specific crowdsourcing platform like Mechanical Turk or Figure Eight. While current platforms are limited in terms of functionality, our goal is to do the best we can with the tools that we have at hand. Independent of the choice, most of the commercial platforms offer the following capabilities:

- a language for coding a task. This is usually performed with HTML-based templates or similar extensions;

- API for integration;

- payments and other incentive mechanisms;

- basic quality control; and

- dashboard for monitoring task progress

The lack of tools and other features should not prevent us from implementing systems that use human computation tasks on production and not for just ad-hoc experimentation. There are some experimental toolkits that help requesters build and deploy HITs. As expressed before, this is a novel area and new systems will emerge in the near future.

When developing a computer program, the programmer must write precise instructions for a machine. In the case of a HIT, code will be executed by a machine in conjunction with a human therefore adding another level of complexity. For the requester, not only does the HIT need to work properly in a machine but it also needs to work for humans. While subtle, this extra consideration should be part of any HIT design.

We will see that there is art in programming HITs, that debugging is difficult, and that requesters need to be open to many strategies and other considerations when implementing such HITs.

There is no established programming language, yet that allows a developer to communicate instructions to a human. The only proven mechanism is to use a language like English in which we can express what we would like another person to do. Because spoken language is ambiguous and has specific characteristics, more than one meaning is possible. Like in any piece of written language that contains instructions, the outcome may not be what we expect. We outline several issues that engineers and developers face when writing software that uses human computation.

"Whoever designed this place is insane"

- Instructions and questions. All HITs require, at some point, a question or a precise instruction about what piece of work is requested and what needs to be done correctly with examples if they are needed. Instructions and questions are very important but, at the same time, workers will not read or remember several pages of details. Asking the right questions, the right way, is part art and part science. We need to be precise and to the point on what is asked and what is expected as a valid answer.

- User interface and content presentation. All the necessary information to perform work in a HIT should be self-contained and presented in a clear manner using standard guidelines. A good interface should help the worker perform work the best way possible. If the worker has problems with a HIT it is highly likely that he/she would move to a different HIT.

- Task difficulty. All human tasks involve a degree of difficulty. Even if we think that the request is very simple, it can have an important cognitive load to the average worker who may struggle to complete the task. It is always desirable to create, if possible, the simplest unit of work that can be performed. We will show how smaller HITs can be composed into a more complex workflow.

- Processing speed. In general, humans are much slower than machines for computing and there is also variation among humans. HITs that are not completed in time or with a high abandonment rate can be an indication of bad design, assignment difficulty, or poor incentives.

- Incentives. Regardless if humans are experts or part of a generic crowdsourced pool, the right cost and incentive structure can help retain and attract good workers. At a minimum, some basic payment structure has to be decided beforehand.

- Errors. Even if we make an effort to address all the previous enumerated issues, it is still possible that we encounter errors in the results, after all, we, humans, are error prone. Certain HITs are very repetitive and after working on several, the task can turn into a very mechanic and dull process. Collecting multiple answers does help to eliminate those errors due to poor attention by workers using different aggregation strategies.

The quality of workers' answers depends on the quality of the HIT. The design is the most important part of the task; no amount of statistical analysis can compensate for a poorly designed survey or questionnaire.

2.3   ASKING QUESTIONS

Requesting a person to perform a function or work is not as precise as instructing a machine like in computer programming where there is a precise general-purpose language and constructions that the programmer needs to follow. With humans, other factors play a role on deciding with respect to following orders.

In general, we are interested in asking the right questions in the best possible possible way. At first, writing a form that asks a question seems like a very simple project but in practice is not so easy. Fortunately, there is existing work in social science and marketing research that can we adapt to our needs.

There are two types of questions: *closed-ended* and *open-ended*. A closed-ended question can normally be answered with a small number of choices (e.g., "yes, maybe, no"). An open-ended question gives the worker the ability to use free-text for responding. In most microtask cases, close-ended questions are the norm. However, there are more sophisticated designs that combine both. It is also possible to instruct a worker to perform a task that does not require the explicit use of a question. That said, the same principles apply to make sure the directions are accurate.

Workers need to understand questions consistently. Furthermore, what constitutes a good answer should be communicated to them. A necessary step is ensuring that all workers have a shared, common understanding of the *meaning* of the question. We have to ask questions that workers are able to answer in the terms required by the question. A question should be as specific as possible and should use words that virtually all workers will understand. There is no need to use special terms unless all workers would be expected to know them or the term is explained in the question.

From a practical stand point, we enumerate the following items of which we should be aware when formulating questions.

- Ask one question at a time. If possible, one concept per question.

- Avoid questions that motivate the worker to respond with we would like to get. These are usually called leading or loaded questions.

- Stay away from using emotional words.

- Prevent the use of ambiguous words. If unavoidable, these keywords need to be defined along with examples whenever possible.

- Use plain English and avoid colloquialisms and jargon. If they are needed, we have to define them.

- Avoid the following words.
  - And. This can signal that we might be combining two questions and asking them as one question.
  - Or. Similar to the previous example, *or* is often associated with a double question.
  - If. The word *if* is often associated with confusing directions or with skip patterns.
  - Not. Avoid using *not* in questions were workers have to respond "yes" or "no"

2.4 COLLECTING RESPONSES

The three most common types of responses are: agreement, evaluation, and frequency.

Agreement asks respondents to the extend that they agree with the question or statement. Agreement is symmetrical around a neutral point and subjects indicate if they agree or not as well as the magnitude of their agreement or disagreement.

```
How do you feel about this social post for the topic XYZ?

() Love it
() Like it
() Neither like it or dislike it
() Dislike it
() Hate it
```

Evaluation asks respondents to rate along a good-bad scale and there is no middle response. The following is a typical relevance evaluation example for assessing query—url pairs.

```
Is this web page relevant to the query XYZ?
```

```
() Perfect
() Excellent
() Good
() Fair
() Bad
```

Frequency asks respondents how often something has happened.

```
How often do you search for product information on the Web?
```

```
() Rarely
() Sometimes
() Most of the time
```

Other ways of collecting answers involve ranking or ordering a set of items and providing responses in narrative or open-ended form.

Information retrieval research often uses a Likert scale or similar to elicit answers. However, the scale is domain dependent, so it is desirable to use one that fits best the task. Cultural differences may make labels confusing; sometimes it is preferable to replace labels with a numeric scale.

Another consideration is to add a separate category, "I do not know" which states that the user clearly does not have the background or experience to answer the question. In the case of relevance assessment this is useful as we are interested in an honest answer and not a guess. Obviously, the number of "I do not know"s for a given task should be low. Some crowdsourcing platforms allow the worker to skip a question, a useful feature as we do not want guesswork.

Equally important is standardizing the responses across workers. That means clearly defining the dimension or continuum respondents are to use in their rating task and giving them a reasonable way to place themselves, or whatever else they are rating, on that continuum. Generally speaking, the more categories workers are asked to use, the better. However, research has shown that most subjects cannot reliably distinguish among more than six or seven levels of response. This can create undesirable cognitive overhead; more options increase the number of decisions a worker must make, and may influence how long it takes to complete the task [79].

Most of us have answered surveys at some point in time and we have probably seen the most common way to pose the agree-disagree task as the following scale: strongly agree, agree, disagree, and strongly disagree. Researchers have pointed out that "strongly" suggests an emotional component, a degree of conviction or caring about the answer over and above the cognitive task that is the central question. Table 2.1 shows a couple of alternatives suggested by Fowler [79]. Survey design literature also recommend to use force-choice rather than agree/disagree as most people will agree with almost any statement.

Table 2.1: Alternatives designs for agree-disagree tasks

Alternative 1	Alternative 2
Completely agree	Completely true
Generally agree	Mostly true
Generally disagree	Mostly untrue
Completely disagree	Completely untrue

2.5   INTERFACE DESIGN

Workers interact with a website or app so it is important to use established usability techniques and related principles for presenting information in a user interface. If the usability of the HIT is low, workers may find it difficult to use and we would end up with no work done which translates to no labels for our models. Analyzing in detail specific user interface guidelines is out of the scope of this book, but some basic design principles to have in mind include the following.

- Accessibility first. The interface needs to be accessible to any worker, anywhere, anytime. The workforce is global and available around the clock.

- Show examples if possible.

- Readability, legibility, and consistency. Workers need to read and understand instructions. Most of relevance tasks require reading text so instructions and content have to be legible.

- Use highlighting, bold, italics, typefaces, and color when needed to improve content presentation. Always make the text clear based on the size, typeface, and spacing of the characters used.

- Minimize the mental effort to accomplish a task. We expect workers to work on many tasks therefore reducing the cognitive load is a goal of the HIT.

We describe now a couple of problematic HIT designs presented in Figures 2.1 and 2.2. In the first one, the task is asking the worker to click on a link and write a description. The video is not embedded in the HIT and it is not clear if the source is spammy or not. Also, this implies that the worker has to watch the video on a different window and get back to the HIT to enter the description. There warnings notes from the requester about work rejection and what is an unacceptable description but never what constitutes a good answer. A better design would be to show the video as part of the HIT and provide generic guidelines on good/bad descriptions instead of a long list of "do not" items.

In the second example, the task also requires the worker to go to a specific website, find specific bits, and then input such information in the form. There are too many instructions for the type of human scrapping that needs to be done. An alternative design would be to show the

Help us describe How-To Videos! Earn $2.50 bonus for every 25 videos entered!

Watch a how-to video, and write a keyword-friendly synopsis describing the video.

1. Click on the link to watch the **Film & Theater** how-to video ==> **332492 Get a 35mm film look with a depth of field adapter**
2. Write a description of the video linked in 4 or more sentences.
3. Be detailed in your description. Describe how the procedure is done.
4. Description should be at least 100 words.
5. Description should be fewer than 2000 characters.
6. Use the character and word counters below to help you stay within the limits.
7. You must complete **25 video descriptions** in order to earn the $2.50 bonus. Bonuses are distributed after HITs have been completed. The more HITs completed and approved, the more you will earn.
8. It is **not** necessary to repeat the headline in your entry. It will **NOT** count toward your word count.
9. Do NOT describe the following: the format, where the video comes from, or how long the video is. This information is **IRRELEVANT**.
10. Do NOT describe the video in the following manner: "She turns around to face the camera. Then she faces left." Follow the examples below.

Current Word Count: 0   Current Character Count: 0 / 2000

Criteria for REJECTION:

1. Entries with obvious and multiple spelling or grammatical errors will be rejected.
2. Entries with fewer than 100 words will be automatically rejected.
3. Text copied from the web or other places will be rejected. Multiple plagiarized answers will lead to being **BLOCKED**. You may use a quotation, but the majority of your content must be **ORIGINAL**.
4. Incomplete and blank answers will be rejected. Multiple blank answers will result in being blocked.
5. Tasks submitted without descriptions will be **rejected**.
6. Tasks submitted with inaccurate descriptions will be **rejected** as well.
7. Do NOT add any personal opinions. Entries with personal opinions or reviews will be automatically **REJECTED**.
8. If you notify us that a link is broken, we appreciate it but will not be able to accept the submission. The notification will result in rejection.
9. Entries that transcribe the video will be **REJECTED**.

Figure 2.1: Example of a problematic design asking to provide a description for video, with a long list of "do not" items and unclear what constitutes good work.

Search for a topic and collect details about advertisers

Go to **www.ezclout.com**. In the Menu on the right side you will find the menu entry "Search" . Click on that Menu Entry which will take you to EZCLOUT's Search Page. Or go **here**. You must use the Search page provided on EZCLOUT's website or your reply will be rejected

Search for "**mustang decal** "

1. Copy the url of the search results here

2. Enter the url of the top placed advertiser

3. Count how many different advertisers are shown on the results page. Include all advertisers (don't forget advertisers at the bottom of the page) If results page does not show advertisers enter "no advertisers". We will verify every answer before we approve your reply.

Figure 2.2: Example of problematic design asking workers to perform quite a bit of work on a specific website and report back.

search results as part of the HIT so the worker can provide the information that is required in the context.

We now show examples of designs that tend to work best. In Figure 2.3, the image is presented to the left and what is needed from the worker in the right side of the screen. The user can zoom in and move the image if needed and some of the fields in the form are already filled in.

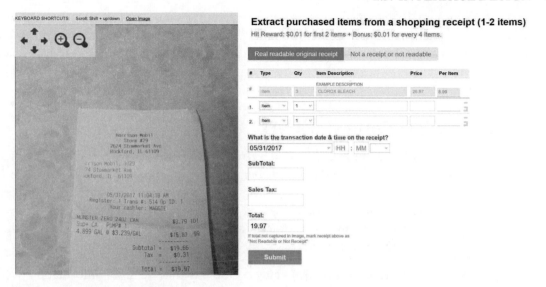

Figure 2.3: Example of a good design. Image is presented on the left and a worker has to provide information on the right.

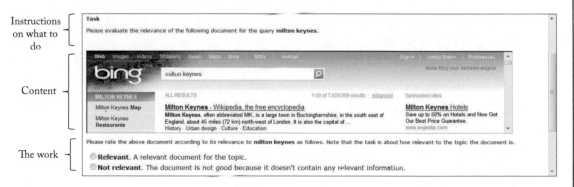

Figure 2.4: Example of a good design. Query, document, and answers are presented inline within the HIT.

Figure 2.4 describes a traditional query-document relevance assessment task. There are three main components presented in sequential order: what needs to be done, the content, and the work answers. While simple, it is surprising to see many HITs that do not show workers all the information that they need in a single place. Often, these HITs require workers to go to another website or specific web property to perform a task and, once they are done, provide the answers.

Our philosophy is that all the necessary information should be presented the best way possible to the worker. As requesters, part of our job is to help the worker the best way possible to accomplish our task. Problematic interfaces can cause work rejection which can discourage workers. McInnis et al. [182] report that workers "express frustration about rejections caused by task or interface mistakes"

2.6   COGNITIVE BIASES AND EFFECTS

We humans can make fast and efficient decisions by using internal short cuts, also known as *cognitive biases*, with the goal of saving time and energy. These short cuts help us provide usually correct judgment but, at the same time, can produce incorrect judgment due to cognitive biases. This is an area of extensive work in psychology and human behavior that we are not going to cover. We briefly outline some examples that we need to be aware when designing HITs as they may have implications in the final output.

- Picture superiority effect and negativity effect. One way that we digest information overload is to skip over things that look ordinary or expected and favor unusual things or of a more negative nature.

- Ambiguity effect. We tend to select options that appear simple or a favorable outcome is known compared to more complex options or unknown outcomes.

- Anchoring effect. The human tendency to rely on the first piece of information offered, when making a decision.

- Bandwagon effect. When there is missing information, individual adoption increases with respect to the proportion who have already done so.

- Hawthorne effect (observer effect). The notion that the mere fact of being observed experimentally can influence the behavior of those being observed.

- Halo effect. The phenomenon that people tend to believe that individuals who have one positive characteristic have other positive qualities.

- Mere exposure effect. The tendency for people to like things the more they are exposed to them (familiarity leads to liking).

- Social desirability. The tendency for people to respond in a socially acceptable direction rather than providing their true feelings.

For example, say that we are interested in comparing the relevance of two search engines, A and B, and we ask workers to select which one is better. If we show workers screenshots from each engine, they would likely select the one that they are most familiar with and would not select the preference more rationally. What we need to do is to de-bias the task. That is, produce a list from each engine without the logo and from any other user interface items (e.g., color, font type, bolding, etc.) that would indicate a particular brand. Workers would then compare two lists that look, in terms of the user interface, exactly the same. The only difference, if visible, would be the relevance ranking of each engine which is exactly what we would like workers to evaluate.

Eickhoff [74] points out that cognitive biases are another form of noise in crowdsourcing and investigates four biases (ambiguity, anchoring, bandwagon, and decoy) in relevance assessment tasks and reports the negative influence that biased labels can have on retrieval evaluation.

2.7 CONTENT ASPECTS

Demographic studies mention entertainment or enjoyment as motivation for working on tasks. It makes sense then to try to design interesting tasks with high quality content. Marshall and Shipman [174] use a similar approach by constructing a realistic set of scenarios for conducting user studies using crowdsourcing. Besides presenting good content, there are aspects like presentation, data familiarity, and task metadata that need to be addressed. A final comment with respect to content is that all information presented in a crowdsourcing experiment is available on the Web so it is expected that no sensitive information should be presented.

2.7.1 PRESENTATION

One important factor is the effect of the user interface on the quality of relevance assessments. This is similar to the finding that generalizt workers may rely on a good document presentation when assessing relevance [133]. Workers in crowdsourcing work fast so instructions have to be clear and with an appropriate reading level, that is, the complexity of words and sentences. This also includes the presentation of quantitative information that may confuse workers (e.g., six vs. half a dozen).

When data sets are very large, even with special filters, it is possible to show adult or inappropriate content by accident. A warning note on the instructions that such content may appear unexpected is also part of a good design.

2.7.2 DATA FAMILIARITY

Gurari et al. [91] investigate the influence of data familiarity in crowdsourcing by studying how workers behavior relates to data of differing levels of familiarity for an image segmentation task. The authors performed three studies in Mechanical Turk: segment everyday vs. biomedical image; segment upright vs. upside down image; and assess segmentation ambiguity. The first study shows evidence that errors are more frequent for everyday images than biomedical images because workers bring more conflicting opinions regarding interpretation. In the second study, workers produce fewer segmentation errors when data is artificially made less familiar. The third experiment shows that workers predict task ambiguity more accurately when data is familiar than unfamiliar.

The takeaway from this work is that data familiarity can lead to better and worse crowd-sourcing results, which is more evidence that human factors do play a substantial role in task design.

2.7.3   METADATA AND INTERNATIONALIZATION

In a crowdsourcing marketplace we compete with other requesters for workers. A clear title, description, and keywords allow potential workers to find our microtasks and preview the content before accepting tasks. It is important then to generate meaningful metadata so workers can search and identify a task in the platform. It is desirable to use a common set of keywords for all the HITs that use the same collection and then specific terms depending on a given run or data subset. Table 2.2 shows such examples for a TREC microtask with three different data sets.

Table 2.2: Generic and data-specific keywords

Dataset	Generic Keywords	Dataset Specific Keywords
D1	Relevance, news articles, TREC	Parkinson's disease, Legionnaires, Greek philosophy, curbing population growth, women clergy
D2	Relevance, news articles, TREC	Child labor, Lyme disease, tourists, violence, ship looses, antibiotics, King Hussein
D3	Relevance, news articles, TREC	Carbon monoxide poisoning, industrial waste disposal, art, suicides, killer bee attacks, birth rates

When there is a need to perform relevance experiments in other languages it is better to fine tune the experiment in English *first* and then localize it to the target language. The first question then is: how do we know if we have enough workers who know a given language? A way to answer that question is to design a simple experiment with some popular content such as Wikipedia with a short topic description in the target language.

2.8   TASK CLARITY

Gadiraju et al. [83] study the role of clarity as a property in crowdsourcing and propose metadata, task type, content, and readability as features for predicting clarity. The notion of clarity is considered in the context of what needs to be produced by a worker (goal clarity) and how such work should be performed (role clarity). Clarity has many implications in task design and work quality. If a task is unclear, workers have to spend extra effort to overcome clarity deficiencies or perform the work without a clear understanding of what is expected. Requesters may not be aware of HIT deficiencies and consider inadequate work related to workers' low performance instead of design defects.

The authors conducted a survey on CrowdFlower and reported that 49% of workers claimed that 30% of tasks that they worked on were unclear. The survey results indicate that a large majority of workers believe that task clarity has a considerable influence on their performance.

2.9 TASK COMPLEXITY

Task complexity has been studied in other areas but has received little attention in crowdsourcing. A requester may have a perception that the task can be performed with some basic knowledge and effort while workers may have a different perspective.

Campbell [43] organizes the various approaches to task complexity according to psychological experience (e.g., enrichment factors, challenge, etc.), task-person interaction (e.g., experience, difficulty, familiarity, etc.), and as a function of objective task characteristics (e.g., information load, constraints, alternatives, etc.). According to Campbell, complex tasks are ill-structured, ambiguous, and usually impose high cognitive demands on the worker.

Robinson [210] proposes a distinction between task complexity, task difficulty, and the interactive conditions under which tasks are performed. Task complexity is the result of the reasoning and demands imposed by the structure of the task. Cognitive simpler and less resource demanding tasks tend to involve a lower error rate and be completed faster. Task difficulty involves the cognitive factors contributing to complexity and affective (e.g., motivation, confidence, etc.) and ability (e.g., aptitude, proficiency, etc.) variables. Task conditions are the interactive demands of the task.

We adopt the distinction proposed by Robinson and categorize crowdsourcing tasks that require effort as follows.

- Complex. The task requires high cognitive load from a worker.

- Difficult. The task requires specific expertise to accomplish the required work.

- Conditions. The task is complex because of low usability or other participatory variables.

As mentioned before, workers interact with a computer system to perform a task and it is recommended to use established user interface design principles to increase the usability of such task. In addition to the task functional inner mechanisms, the clarity of instructions and proper content presentation should not only make the task more usable but also appeal to workers.

We humans have a short-term working memory and many studies have shown that anything that adds demands on the working memory has a cost in terms of attention. From a Human-Computer Interaction (HCI) view, the advice is that all necessary information should be provided in the interface with the goal of minimizing the short-term memory load. HITs that require workers to go to other Internet services and copy/paste information or demand workers to choose from a long list of categories or options are examples that we should not follow. Besides HCI recommendations, partitioning a HIT into smaller ones is also a viable option as we will see in other examples in the rest of the book.

Tasks with low usability and high cognitive load can be improved by following established HCI guidance. With expertise, the problem is different. We are interested in qualified workers that can perform well in our task. In some cases, workers may find that a particular topic or data set requires more expertise or a specific skill set to correctly answer a question. In other words, we should also think of certain tasks as more difficult than others, therefore workers may have problems providing answers.

The work by Yang et al. [256] is one of the first attempts at understanding the complexity of crowdsourcing tasks. They model complexity using metadata, content, and visual features derived from task structure. Actions like copy/paste are perceived as simple compared to search/find which are more demanding.

Abraham et al. [1] analyzed a real-world data set of 250,000 answers from UHRS, Microsoft's in-house crowdsourcing platform, and made two empirical observations. First, the difficulty of a random HIT is distributed near-uniformly across a wide range. Second, they investigated the interplay between HIT difficulty and worker quality, and found that high-quality workers are significantly better than low-quality workers for the relatively harder tasks, whereas there is very little difference between all workers for the relatively easy tasks. The main takeaway is that the difference in performance between good and bad workers is much more significant for harder HITs than for easier HITs.

Related to complexity is measuring the effort that a task requires from workers to complete. An example of such is the NASA-TLX index used for assessing workloads. Cheng et al. [49] propose the error time area (ETA) to measure crowdsourcing effort. The ETA metric computes quality as a function of task duration and can be used to estimate the task's fair price.

2.10 SENSITIVE DATA

So far, we've seen examples where the data is either publicly available or contains very little delicate information. Unfortunately, in enterprise scenarios most of the data is sensitive but also with many levels of access control mechanisms. A similar scenario is personalized information with respect to Internet services and products. Regulations like GDPR enforce service providers to implement data collection, consent, and anonymization, to name a few.

There is little work on labeling sensitive or personalized data. Moving away from the privacy considerations, one of the biggest problems with labeling and evaluating personal information is the lack of context. One solution is to use a "bring your own network" approach. That is, workers can evaluate their own content only. An obvious problem is that it is very difficult to implement as it requires a representative sample of real users who are willing to label. A different solution described by Pantel et al. [195], in the context of social annotations, is to construct an artificial social network (e.g., friends and content) so any worker can perform the task.

2.11   EXAMPLES

In this section, we present five different HIT designs that showcase common scenarios found in information retrieval that can also be adapted to other areas. We start with a traditional TREC-style binary relevance assessment task, expand it to graded relevance assessment, and perform another iteration for Web search relevance assessment. We then describe a survey-like HIT where the goal is to capture user input data. Finally, moving away from documents and queries, we tap into social data and show a HIT with a user study focus.

We use the following convention in the HIT source code: $DOCUMENT$ denotes the variable DOCUMENT that gets instantiated at run time, () a radio button, [] a check-box, and [InputBox] a text input field.

2.11.1   BINARY RELEVANCE ASSESSMENT

In TREC, relevance assessments are performed by hired editors and the instructions are very technical [243]. If we look at a specific track like Ad-hoc, the original instructions are four pages long, making it somewhat difficult to present them in a web user interface.

Using the Ad-hoc track instructions as a baseline[1] and extracting what we believe are the most salient parts, we designed the following HIT for assessing the relevance of a document to a given query. The instructions and descriptions are in context, as shown in the example with the topic space program, with binary options. One disadvantage with this implementation is that the topic description, while useful, takes up significant real estate. Once the worker is familiar with the task, the text is somewhat redundant.

```
Document Relevance Evaluation

Instructions

Evaluate the relevance of a document to the space program topic. A document
is relevant if it would be useful if you were writing a report on the space
program topic. Each document should be judged on its own merits. That is, a
document is still relevant even if it is the thirtieth document you have
seen with the same information.

Tips
- Payment based on quality of the work completed. Please follow the
  instructions.
- Be consistent in your judgments.
- A document should not be judged as relevant or irrelevant based only on
```

[1]Ellen Voorhees, Personal communication, 2011.

```
      the title of the document. You must read the document
```

```
Task
```

```
Please evaluate the relevance of the following document about the space
program topic. To be relevant, a document must discuss the goals or plans
of a space program or space project and identify the organization(s)
sponsoring the program. The space program is a coherent set of initiatives
to exploit outer space. The space project is a specific mission to exploit
outer space.
```

```
$DOCUMENT$
```

```
Please rate the above document according to its relevance to the space
program topic as follows. Note that the task is about how relevant to the
topic the document is.
```

```
() Relevant. A relevant document for the topic.
() Not relevant. The document is not good because it doesn't contain any
   relevant information.
```

2.11.2 GRADED RELEVANCE ASSESSMENT

In the follow-up design, we introduce three modifications. First, we remove the topic description and make the instructions more generic. Second, graded relevance with four categories in replacement of binary assessments. Third, a free-form and non-mandatory input text is added in case the worker would like to provide more information for a given answer.

```
Document Relevance Evaluation
```

```
Instructions
```

```
Evaluate the relevance of a document to the given topic. A document is
relevant if it would be useful if you were writing a report on such topic.
Each document should be judged on its own merits. That is, a document
is still relevant even if it is the thirtieth document you have seen with
the same information.
```

```
Tips
```

- Payment is based on quality of the work completed. Please follow the
  instructions.
- Be consistent in your judgments.
- A document should not be judged as relevant or irrelevant based only
  on the title of the document. You must read the document.

Task

Please evaluate the relevance of the following document about $TOPIC$.

$DOCUMENT$

Please rate the above document according to its relevance to $TOPIC$ as
follows. Note that the task is about how relevant to the topic the
document is.

() Excellent. The document discusses the themes of the topic exhaustively.
() Good. The document contains information but the presentation is not
   exhaustive or there might be a better document.
() Fair. The document only points to the topic. It does not contain more
   information than the topic description or portions of the text are
   inaccurate.
() Not relevant. The document is not good because it does not contain any
   relevant information.

Please justify your answer. We appreciate your comments.

[InputBox]

2.11.3 WEB PAGE RELEVANCE ASSESSMENT

The third installment for relevance assessment involves web pages where the goal is to label how
relevant a page is to a given query. The instructions are straightforward with some changes in
the categories. Note that the emphasis is more on the utilitarian value of the page as opposed to
the notion of a topic like in the previous examples. Absent from this HIT are specific guidelines
for adult and offensive content, which are company specific.

Search Engine Relevance Evaluation

```
Please look at this web page and answer how relevant it is to the query.

Task

How relevant is the following webpage to the query $QUERY$.

$WEBPAGE$

() Perfect. Exactly and completely what the user wanted, there could be no
   better result.
() Excellent. Exactly what the user wanted, but there may be other results
   that as good or better
() Good. Mostly what the user wanted, but not exactly.
() Fair. Loosely related to what the user wanted.
() Bad. Certainly not what the user wanted

Please let us know if you have any comments.

[InputBox]
```

2.11.4 RANKED COMPARISON

A very popular mechanism for selecting a preference is to compare two items and let workers decide which one is best. We are all familiar with a blind taste test, where we have to pick one of two sodas without knowing the brand in advance. A key feature of this type of designs is randomization. That is, the brands (e.g., ranking functions, search engine, etc.) are assigned at random.

In our example, we are interested in evaluating the performance of two different search engines. It could be two competitors, two different ranking functions that we are testing, or two different ways of presenting the same information. In any case, the A-B comparison HIT shows the results from two different sources for a given query. The worker needs to select A or B and, in that case, that the worker sees no difference, a third alternative. The design is simple and works well in practice, as shown in the screenshot in Figure 2.5.

```
Which search result is better?

Please take a look the following 2 search results for the given query and
let us know which one is better.
```

```
Query: $QUERY$

Search engine A        Search engine B

$SearchResultsFromA$ $SearchResultsFromB$

Based on the information presented above, which result is better for the
query $QUERY$?

() A is better.
() B is better.
() They are the same.
```

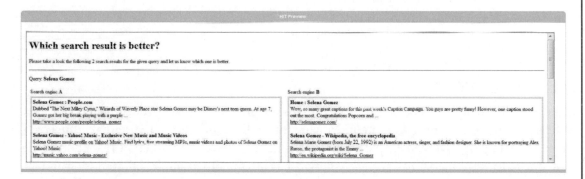

Figure 2.5: A-B comparison HIT example. The worker has to select which of the two de-branded search engine results list is better.

2.11.5 SURVEY STYLE

There are many cases where we would like to collect user data and a survey-style HIT should do the work. In this particular example, we would like users to volunteer a query that they have issued in any search engine and some extra information about the intent by marking some categories with check-boxes ([]). Note that instead of asking them to provide the intent in the form of a free-text input box, we have pre-categorized the answers to speed up the process. The worker only needs to type the query and select the closest category.

```
Describe a search you conducted recently
```

```
This is a survey about a search you conducted recently in a search engine.

1. Please enter a query (keywords or terms you type into a search box)
   that you used, exactly the way you used it.

[InputBox]

2. How would you categorize what you were trying to do (select all that
    apply)?

[] Research a topic
[] Navigate to a specific website
[] Find out about a breaking news story
[] Quickly find or check on a specific reference or fact
[] Find map or location information
[] Buy or research a product or service
[] Other not described by any of the above
```

2.11.6 USER STUDY

The previous example were about somewhat well-known search scenarios: document assessment, relevance evaluation, and query intent. Moving into a different source, Twitter data, the goal is to get a feeling of how workers perceive a tweet. Because tweets are different from documents and due to the exploratory nature of the study, the HIT contains examples of interesting and uninteresting tweets. Considering that tweets are much smaller than a document, the HIT groups five tweets together.

```
What do you think of the following tweets?

Please read the tweets below and mark them as "interesting" or "not
interesting". "Not interesting" tweets include advertisements, opinions
and trivial updates about daily life.  "Interesting" tweets should mention
specific information that people might care about.  Here are a few
examples:

Interesting:

- Another earthquake hits Haiti.
- No source, but allegedly #TonightShow staffers upset with Conan.
```

```
http://tinyurl.com/ybts7sm
```
- Google Threatens to Pull out of China because of Cyber Attacks
  & Censorship.

```
Not interesting:
```

- Going for lunch with my friend.
- Make more money as a copywriter than you ever thought possible!
- I love the Simpsons, but can't stand the musical episodes

```
Tip: Some tweets will be hard to label.  When in doubt, label a tweet
uninteresting. Please try to be consistent.
```

```
Task
```

```
Please mark if these tweets are interesting or not. Feel free to give us
more feedback at the end.
```

```
$Tweet1$ () Interesting () Not interesting
$Tweet2$ () Interesting () Not interesting
$Tweet3$ () Interesting () Not interesting
$Tweet4$ () Interesting () Not interesting
$Tweet5$ () Interesting () Not interesting
```

```
Please let us know if you have comments. We appreciate your feedback
for this study.
```

```
[InputBox]
```

2.12 SUMMARY

Crowdsourcing offers flexibility to design and implement different types of tasks. However, implementing a good HIT requires effort that goes beyond a simple form for data entry. HITs have to be designed carefully to achieve good results.

In the real world, when there are problems with a HIT, the first reaction is to "fix the instructions". Unfortunately, the so-called "instructions" tend to balloon in terms of examples and special cases making it several pages long. While the requester may think the problem has been corrected because of the new instructions, in reality, workers do not read lengthy documentation. After all, who reads instruction manuals?

The delicate balance of asking the right question with sufficient contextual information that does not overwhelm workers is one of the most difficult parts of designing good HITs. The words in a HIT should be chosen so that all workers understand their meaning and all workers have the same sense of what the meaning is. If what is requested is too complex to be included in a single question, we probably need to ask multiple questions or partition the HIT as we will see in other chapters. Finally, cognitive biases can introduce noise in the results.

Pointers

The books by Fowler [79], Bradburn et al. [30], and Rosenthal and Rosnow [212] provide standard guidelines for survey and questionnaire design. Spector's monograph covers the necessary steps for developing summated rating sacles [227]. Deming describes types of survey errors and biases in [62].

There are other books that cover many aspects of HCI and describe important principles that can be applied when designing HITs [140, 159, 187].

CHAPTER 3

Quality Assurance

> The object of taking data is to provide a basis for action.
>
> W. Edwards Deming

We take an inclusive view for quality instead of focusing on just low-performance workers. We present a framework for managing quality and task development, including HIT design, assessment of the workers and their work, and statistical methods for measuring reliability. Some of these techniques are platform independent and can be used in different scenarios. In other cases, specific features are available as part of the service.

3.1 QUALITY FRAMEWORK

Quality control in crowdsourcing systems, a critical issue in practice, is an active area of research. From the requester's point of view, it is well known that the output delivered by the crowd needs to be checked for quality since the results are produced by workers with a wide range of abilities, expertise, and motivation. However, focusing only on worker's performance is just one of the many aspects that we need to comprehend when managing quality in crowdsourcing.

But before we venture further we need to ask the following obligatory question: what do we mean by quality in crowdsourcing? We follow the *meets internal customer needs* definition for quality, that is, the extent to which the results meet or exceed requesters' requirements or expectations.

There is previous work on framing quality control in crowdsourcing and we examine briefly a couple of proposed taxonomies. The work by Allahbakhsh et al. [2] characterizes quality along two main dimensions: workers' profile and task design. Due to the importance of workers' abilities, reputation and expertise are significant attributes in the profile. For task design, the following factors contribute to quality: definition or instructions, user interface, granularity, and incentives. More recently, Daniel et al. [56] proposes a more comprehensive taxonomy that focuses on three main categories—quality model, assessment (measures and methods), and assurance (actions to achieve levels of quality)—and each category is divided into sub-categories. Quality model is expanded to dimensions (data, task, people) and attributes; quality assessment is split into techniques (individual, group, computation-based) and assessment methods; and quality assurance dissected into strategies (data, task, people) and actions.

Given our interest in implementation and scalability, we envision two complementary views with respect to quality: the quality of the *module* (HIT, worker, data), m_q, and the quality of the results that the module can produce, w_q, as presented in Figure 3.1. This separation of concerns allows us to initially focus our energy on implementing a solid working module first that produces good results taking into account feedback and incrementally iterate over time to improve the quality of new work. We can start with a simple technique for work quality and later replace it with a more advanced algorithm. There are trade-offs and design decisions that depend on cost and platform ownership when adopting more sophisticated techniques. In this chapter, we cover module quality and in the next one we describe the many techniques for work quality.

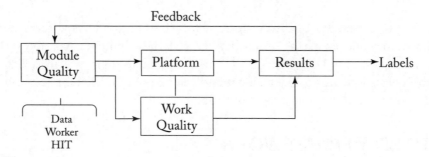

Figure 3.1: Two-phase quality control framework. Module quality enables developers to concentrate on a reliable working HIT first and later test different techniques for work quality. The feedback loop here can be either explicit from workers or derived from the results.

3.2   QUALITY CONTROL OVERVIEW

Quality control is a key part of a HIT. If the HIT produces low-quality results, the labels would be inferior and therefore our models would learn the wrong things. Quality should be applied across all aspects of task design, and not just limited to choosing workers and vetting their work. For example, seemingly simple factors such as the quality of the instructions and the presentation of objects (e.g., documents, images, etc.) have significant impact on the results. The user interface should make workers' tasks easier not more difficult. As workers go through tasks, diversity of topics in a single run can help avoid stalling the HIT due to lack of interest. While it is always possible to detect bad workers, at the same time, the requester can be acquiring a bad reputation among workers. We may think the worker is doing a bad job but, at the same time, the same worker may think we are a lousy requester.

Who is responsible for ensuring high quality? Should commercial platforms manage and control all quality-related issues to make sure requesters get only the best results? Or, should a requester handle such supervision? Managing the quality of the work and overall worker performance is difficult and the answer lies in between: we should expect some basic features provided by platforms and plan for computing additional checks depending on the complexity of the task at hand.

Platform features like spam detection and basic worker performance statistics are useful at the beginning for vetting purposes but they may not be sufficient to enforce good work. In several cases, the problem is that workers may not have the expertise required to perform the task.

"I'm searching on 'precooked meat product,'
but all I'm getting is spam."

In general, if a gold standard exists it is possible to compare the performance of workers against experts in such set. For those cases where no gold standard set is available, worker aggregation and majority voting should work.

When should we enforce quality? Quality control is an on-going activity so the answer is *always*: *before* we start the main tasks by recruiting and qualifying the right workers, *during* the time workers are executing on the task by rewarding (or penalizing), and *after* the task is completed by computing accuracy and correctness.

The crowd is globally diverse, both in its skill set and behavior. Participants may be willing to work but incompetent, they may be competent but lazy, ethical but distracted by their surrounding environment, or they may simply be out there to maximize their income through cheating [126]. There is also a possible mismatch between the motivations of the requesters and that of the crowds [220].

For example, some workers may be more inclined to complete as many HITs as possible within the shortest time to maximize their income, to the possible detriment of the quality of their work [124]. Worker anonymity in some crowdsourcing platforms can further exacerbate the problem [230], reducing the perceived risk of punishment for bad work. As a result, cheating and random behavior among workers has been studied [125, 261].

3.3   RECOMMENDATIONS FROM PLATFORMS

Publicly available information about platform quality control mechanisms is insufficient due to proprietary considerations. This is unlikely to change as quality is a major product advantage when deciding which service to use.

Mechanical Turk provides API documentation that includes generic guidelines and use cases.[1] A good recommendation from Amazon is to test HITs on the Mechanical Turk sandbox to make sure the basic functionality works before publishing the task on the marketplace. Master workers, a selection of workers who have demonstrated the ability to provide successful results for specific types of tasks across multiple tasks, are also an alternative for identifying high-performance workers.

CrowdFlower describe a number of case studies on content moderation, data categorization, data collection, image annotation, search relevance, sentiment analysis, and transcription.[2] The company summarizes their overall quality control approach as follows:[3]

- Encourage users to write clear tasks through templates and widgets. Requesters can get feedback from the crowd before the task runs.

- Hiding in questions where the user also puts the answer and a reason for the answer.

- Global reputation system that includes how long someone has been on the platform and how accurate they have generally been. Higher reputation workers make a lot more money so workers care a lot about their reputation.

- Skills system where workers can qualify for skills.

- Aggregating multiple judgments, typically weighting based on reputation.

Most of the platforms provide features for blocking workers from tasks and rejecting individual assignments. That being said, it is easier to blame workers for incorrect answers when probably the interface was confusing, instructions were not clear, payment was inadequate, or it was a bad design.

3.4   WORKER QUALIFICATION

How do we qualify a worker? A possible filter for selecting good workers is to use the *approval rate*. The approval rate is a metric provided by Mechanical Turk that measures the overall rating of each worker in the system. Amazon defines the metric as the percentage of assignments the worker has submitted that were subsequently approved by the requester, over all assignments the worker has submitted.

However, using very high approval rates decreases the worker population available and may increase the time necessary to complete the evaluation. Kazai compared different groups

---

[1]https://aws.amazon.com/documentation/mturk/
[2]https://www.crowdflower.com/use-cases/
[3]Lukas Biewald, Personal communication, 2017.

of workers in Mechanical Turk and found that more qualified workers (i.e., higher acceptance rate) produce better quality results [124].

It is possible to control work quality by using *qualification tests*. A qualification test is a set of questions (like a HIT) that the worker must answer to qualify and therefore work on the assignments. After seeing the preview, workers can choose to accept the task where, optionally, they must pass a *qualification exam* to be officially assigned the task.

A qualification test is a much better quality filter but also involves more development cycles. In the case of relevance evaluation it is somewhat difficult to test relevance. What we propose is to generate questions about the topics so workers can get familiar with the content before performing the tasks, even if they search online for a particular answer.

It is also possible, however, for a worker to pass the test and then be lazy for the rest of the task. A drawback of using qualification tests is that workers may not feel like performing work that requires a test. Tasks that require a qualification test also take longer to complete. Finally, there is a hidden cost: the test has to be developed and maintained over time. Below are some examples of potential questions for a test.

```
1.  Please identify the main topic of the following text:

Malaysia's bid to launch its first satellite has encountered a hitch as
Intelsat, a United States-based satellite operator, has also applied
for the same orbital slot. Energy, Telecommunications, and Posts
Minister Datuk Sri Samy Vellu said Intelsat has applied to the
International Telecommunications Union [ITU] to position its satellite
at the 91.5 degree east orbital slot just as Malaysia had done for its
Malaysia East Asia Satellite [Measat].

[] Space program
[] Satellite launch
[] Moon exploration
[] International Space Station
[] Mars landing

2.  Please identify the main topic of the following text:

The U.S. military said Friday reports that as many as 147 civilians died
in fighting involving involving American forces and the Taliban were
``extremely over-exaggerated'' and investigators were still analyzing
the data collected at the site. In the south, meanwhile, four NATO
soldiers and 21 civilians died in a string of insurgent attacks, and an
```

```
unmanned U.S. drone crashed in central Ghazni province.

[] USA
[] Taliban
[] NATO
[] All of the above
[] None of the above
```

When the goal of the test is to measure knowledge, some other considerations are important. For example:

- consider whether the level of difficulty of the knowledge question is appropriate for the purposes of the task;
- if yes-no questions are appropriate, ask several on the same topic to reduce the likelihood of successful guessing; and
- use images and other nonverbal procedures for determining knowledge.

The obvious advantages of qualification tests are that they are a good tool for controlling the quality of new hired workers. The disadvantages are a bit more numerous. There is extra cost involved to design and implement the test. Besides development, the test has to be maintained over time. For subjective tasks, qualification tests may not work. Finally, tests may turn off workers and hurt the overall completion time.

If a requester is going to be very strict about worker qualification and overall performance, we should expect the same about workers' opinions of a requester. Unfortunately, there is little infrastructure available for that, except for a few early prototypes and websites that track bad requesters. We should treat our workers with respect and professionally: pay on time, pay what we think the task is worth rather than the minimum, and provide them with clear instructions and content so they can complete the task the best way possible. While it is possible that some people may try to game the system, we believe that, in general, workers act on good faith.

Downs et al. [71] explore a screening task that consists of a simple question followed by a difficult one. There was no required knowledge to answers those questions and getting either wrong is an indication that the worker may not be suitable for the task. Another alternative proposed by Law et al. [149] is to ask workers to choose tasks for which they have expertise, interest, and confidence.

We describe more techniques for expertise detection and user selection on the next chapter.

3.5 RELIABILITY AND VALIDITY

Data is the new oil and therefore it must be trusted. In other words, data should be of high quality, reliable, and should mean the same for everyone who uses it. All measurements are subject to errors that can affect the reliability and validity of the experiments or microtasks.

In statistics, there are standards to assess reliability and validity in different situations and we will provide a brief overview of the main concepts adapted from behavioral research and content analysis. We are interested in consistency across raters and consistency across responses.

We follow the same definitions provided by Rosenthal and Rosnow [212] for reliability and validity: *reliability* is the degree to which observations or measures are consistent, repeatable, or stable and *validity* is the degree to which what is observed or measured is the same as what was purported to be observed or measured.

Data is reliable if workers agree on the assessments or answers they have to provide. If different workers produce consistently similar results, then they have understood the instructions and it is expected that they should perform consistently. Validity refers to how well a test or rating scale measures what is it supposed to measure.

Reliability in research implies repeatability, that is, replication of experiment results across time and across different measures and observers. We define an experiment as a test or series of tests and to understand the functioning of such test, we must understand its reliability. A test-retest reliability refers to the temporal stability of a test from one measurement session to another.

We now look at the reliability of workers and the reliability of test components or internal consistency.

3.5.1   INTER-RATER RELIABILITY

If two or more workers agree on a judgment, the higher the chances are that the label is correct. Inter-rater reliability measures the extent to which independent judges (workers in our case) evaluate or assess an object and reach the same conclusion. That is, consistent results from different observers who are measuring the same item. In general, if workers are not consistent then there is usually a problem with them or the instructions are of inferior quality.

The following are the main statistics that researchers and practitioners use to describe inter-rater reliability. The survey by Artstein and Poesio [13] covers each of them and variations in more detail.

- Percentage agreement. This method calculates the cases that received the same rating by two judges and divides the number by the total number of cases rated by the two judges. Let N represent the total number of subjects, n the number of ratings per subject and k the number of categories into which assignments are made.

  P_o is observed agreement and P_o is observed disagreement. P_e is expected agreement and P_e is expected disagreement:

$$agreement_i = \begin{cases} 1 & \text{if the two judges assign } i \text{ to the same category} \\ 0 & \text{if the two judges assign } i \text{ to different categories} \end{cases}$$

$$P_o = \frac{1}{i} \sum_{i \in I} agreement_i$$

This method calculates the cases that received the same rating by two judges and divides that number by the total number of cases rated by the two judges. An advantage is that it is easy to compute and intuitive to interpret. While is a common practice to report inter-rater agreement as a percentage, there is consensus in the literature that this is a misleading statistic as it fails to differentiate between accuracy and variability, therefore overestimating true inter-rater agreement.

- Cohen's kappa (κ), a chance-adjusted measure of agreement. This statistic was designed to estimate the degree of consensus between two judges by correcting if they are operating by chance alone. The coefficient is computed using the following formula:

$$\kappa = \frac{P_o - P_e}{1 - P_e}$$

where $P_e = \sum_k p_{Ak} p_B k$, p_{Ak} is the proportion of the value k used by judge A, and p_{Bk} is the proportion of value k used by the other judge B.

- Fleiss' kappa (κ). A generalization of Cohen's kappa (κ) for n raters.

- Krippendorff's alpha (α). The coefficient α is calculated by looking at the overall distribution of judges regardless on which judge produced the judgments [139]:

$$\alpha = 1 - \frac{D_o}{1 - D_e}$$

When agreement is observed to be perfect and disagreement is absent, $D_o = 0$ and $\alpha = 1$, indicating perfect reliability.

3.5.2   INTERNAL CONSISTENCY

Internal consistency means getting consistent results from different parts of a measure. That is, the degree to which different parts of a test are measuring the same thing. For reliability of a test components or internal consistency, there are three main statistics

- Split-half. The split-half reliability method randomly splits the data set into two comparable halves and the scores on the halves are then correlated. A score for each participant is then calculated based on each half of the scale. If a scale is reliable a person's score on one half of the scale should be the same (or similar) to their score on the other half. The correlation between the two halves is the statistic computed in the split-half method, with large correlation being a sign of reliability. A problem with this technique is that different split-halves can give different estimates of internal consistency.

- Kuder-Richardson (KR-20) formula:

$$r_u = (\frac{n}{n-1})(\frac{\sigma_t^2 - \sum PQ}{\sigma_t^2})$$

where r_u = the reliability coefficient; n = number of items in the test; and σ_t^2 = total variance of the test P = proportions of correct responses to each item Q = 1- P. KR-20 is used for measures with dichotomous choices.

- Cronbach's alpha α. Cronbach's alpha is more general as it takes the average of all possible split-halves and can be used for continuous and dichotomous scores:

$$\alpha = (\frac{k}{k-1})(1 - \frac{\sum_{i=1}^{k} \sigma_{y_i}^2}{\sigma_x^2})$$

where k = number of items; $\sigma_{y_i}^2$ is the variance associated with i, and σ_x^2 the variance associated with the observed total items.

3.5.3 DISCUSSION

What does all of the above mean and which statistic should we use? The practical recommendation is to use an inter-rater statistic that best fits the task and the designer's goals and avoid percentage agreement. Modern statistical software supports most of the inter-rater statistics like the packages psy and irr in R.

An inter-rater statistic produces a value between -1 and 1, where 1 is perfect agreement, 0 is due to chance, and -1 means total lack of agreement. The interpretation of the values is more tricky. Table 3.1, adapted from Landis and Koch [146], shows labels assigned to corresponding κ ranges as *recommendations* for interpreting such values. Krippendorff suggests relying on measures of $\alpha > 0.8$ and considers measures between $\alpha = 0.6$ and $\alpha = 0.8$ only for drawing tentative conclusions. For κ, acceptable values are > 0.7, which indicates substantial strength.

All these recommendations are appropriate for content analysis, and biomedical and educational research but are not realistic for the type of microtasks that are usually implemented in crowdsourcing. Reidsma and Carletta [209] argue that machine learning applications can tolerate data with low reliability if rater disagreement looks like random noise. Passonneau and Carpenter [201] dispute that high inter-rater agreement is "neither necessary nor sufficient to ensure high quality gold-standard labels" and show a case study of word sense annotation using an expectation maximization model [58].

In general, a high value for κ (or α) is not enough to guarantee reliability as disagreement may not be random. In practice, we should expect κ values in the fair and moderate range and use contingency tables to inspect for annotator's bias.

Table 3.1: Relative strength of agreement associated with κ values (adapted from [146])

κ	Strength of Agreement
< 0	Poor
0.00 – 0.20	Slight
0.21 – 0.40	Fair
0.41 – 0.60	Moderate
0.61 – 0.80	Substantial
0.81 – 1.00	Almost perfect

3.6   HIT DEBUGGING

The statistical techniques that we have described in the previous section are helpful for measuring the reliability of the results under the assumption that the HIT is bug-free. If the inter-rater agreement in the results is low, is that because workers are not performing as expected or a sign that our HIT is defective? How do we measure the quality of a HIT? More importantly, how do we debug a HIT?

In general, human computation tasks are difficult to debug because there are three main contingent factors: the workers, the task design, and the data that needs to be labeled. The challenge is how to identify the factor that is causing low-quality results.

We illustrate the problem by designing a HIT for a tweet classifier [5] and introducing a debugging pattern. The first HIT design consists of asking workers to mark if a tweet is interesting or not, following the example described in Section 2.11.6. Because the notion of "interestingness" is somewhat vague, the instructions are limited and therefore we relied on workers' judgments. When computing inter-rater agreement, κ values were in the moderate range so it was unclear what the problem was. Spammy workers? Biased data set? Wrong task design? How can we do better?

An obvious follow-up is to use a more aggressive worker inspection mechanism to weed out low performance or change the platform. Another alternative is to re-evaluate the HIT and try a different task design. Perhaps the way the HIT was implemented is not the appropriate one for our needs.

```
Tweet classification

Please read the tweets below and mark the ones that you think are
interesting. You can mark more than one. Also, if you think that none
of them are interesting, please don't make any selections.
```

```
Tip: Some tweets will be hard to label.  Please try to be consistent.

Task: Please mark the tweets that you think are interesting. Feel free to
give us more feedback in the box near the respective tweet.

[] $Tweet1$ [InputBox]
[] $Tweet2$ [InputBox]
[] $Tweet3$ [InputBox]
[] $Tweet4$ [InputBox]
[] $Tweet5$ [InputBox]
```

One plan of attack for debugging is to use a "data-worker-task" pattern where the aim is to dive into each of the three contingent factors with the end goal of debugging (and fixing) each potential problem. A component of the pattern is to include in the HIT specialized within-task Human Intelligence Data-Driven Enquiries (HIDDEN) that support quality control while allowing the task to be performed reliably in the absence of a gold set [6]. The HIT is augmented with a couple of extra questions with the goal of identifying low performance workers, as presented in Figure 3.2. We can think of Q1 as the algorithmic HIDDEN whereas Q2 is more semantic and both answers can be produced offline before making the data set available. Q3 is the question that we use to collect labels. By maintaining high inter-rater agreement on the HIDDENs we can iterate and debug a potentially problematic question, in our case Q3.

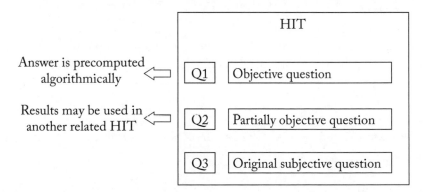

Figure 3.2: Basic structure of HIDDEN at work. Q1 is a structural task with a computable answer that may inform data science or analytics questions; Q2 may be designed to be useful for another application; and Q3 is the original subjective judgment.

The re-designed HIT contains three questions. Questions Q1 and Q2 comprise the HIDDENs and Q3, the actual tweet that is assessed. To demonstrate the technique, let's use one of the most popular tweets of all time by Ellen DeGeneres (@TheEllenShow):

If only Bradley's arm was longer. Best photo ever. #oscars
pic.twitter.com/C9U5NOtGap

For Q1, the hashtag count is easily computable and for Q2, a named-entity recognizer should tag "Bradley" as a person type. Thus, the pre-computed answers for the HIDDENs, for the above example, are 1 and Yes, respectively.

How interesting is a Tweet?

You will be asked 3 questions about the tweet you see below.

In the first question, please tell us how many hashtagged words (words that begin with a "#") are in the tweet. For example, the tweet "All beef products must be tested for #horsemeat by next Friday after reports of #Findus contamination" contains 2 hashtagged words.

In the second question, please tell us if the tweet contains the name of a specific person. For example, the tweet "Kellogg recalls cereal over risk of glass fragments" DOES NOT name a specific person (Kellogg is a company, not a person). The tweet "Is Daniel Day-Lewis the best actor of all time?" DOES name a specific person (Daniel Day-Lewis is a person). Names that are preceded by an "@" don't count. In other words the tweet "Earth-Like Planets May Be "Next Door" in Milky Way via @NedPotterABC" DOES NOT name a specific person.

In the third question, you will be asked to judge whether or not the tweet is interesting. Please try to be consistent with your answers.

$Tweet$

Q1. How many hashtagged words (words that begin with a "#") are in this tweet?

() 0 (no hashtags)
() 1
() 2
() 3 or more

Q2. Does the tweet name a specific person?

() Yes

```
() No
```

```
Q3. Do you think the tweet is interesting to a broad audience?
```

```
() Yes
() No
```

By running the HIT and analyzing the results, the inter-rater agreement for Q1 (κ = 0.91, α = 0.91) and Q2 (κ = 0.771, α = 0.771) indicates that worker performance is not the problem. However, the inter-rater agreement for the main question, Q3 (κ = 0.033, α = 0.035), is very low which indicates that there is a problem with this question.

What's going on? How can we improve Q3? So far, we have modeled Q3 in a *labels for the machine* style. That is, our classifier requires binary labels and that is what we ask workers. While this is very practical, maybe the workers would prefer different options for answering our question. An alternative would be to widen the scale and use human-friendly categories, that is, *labels for humans*. The newly improved HIT template contains more choices for Q3. Compared to the previous design, the six elements are independent and multiple descriptors can be chosen if the worker thinks that more than one apply to the tweet.

We are providing a different scale that, if it works, can produce better quality results. A mapping from this new set of answers to a binary form is still needed for our classifier.

```
Q1. How many hashtagged words (words that begin with a "#") are in
    this tweet?
```

```
() 0 (no hashtags)
() 1
() 2
() 3 or more
```

```
Q2. Does the tweet name a specific person?
```

```
() Yes
() No
```

```
Q3. Please check all the boxes that apply to this tweet.
```

```
[] Worthless
[] Trivial
[] Funny
```

```
[] Makes me curious
[] Contains useful information
[] Important news
```

Running the HIT again and analyzing the results, the inter-rater agreement for Q1 (α = 0.910) and Q2 (α = 0.758) remains high as expected. By computing inter-rater agreement per each category for Q3, we can observe that certain categories provide more signal than others. These are the values for the six categories in Q3: Worthless (α = 0.384), Trivial (α = 0.097), Funny (α = 0.134), Makes me curious (α = 0.056), Contains useful information (α = 0.079), and Important news (α = 0.314).

We do not claim that the above HIT example is completely bug free nor that the above categories are the best for the task. The α values are still low, however they can be improved over time. We just showed the proposed pattern in action as a reusable solution to identify a problematic factor and how, after introducing a fix, the statistics show the effect of such change.

To summarize the debugging strategy, we provide the following.

- Data. We first start with the data (the work to be done) with the aim of reducing the subjectivity of the data and narrowing the data genre. Many factors can cause bias on the workers and reducing the range on these factors can make the final results more accurate.

- Workers. We then look at the performance of the workers in the absence of a gold set or high inter-rater agreement. A CAPTCHA-like technique called HIDDEN is useful for solving this problem. Instead of asking a completely orthogonal question like the traditional CAPTCHAs, the questions are designed to focus the workers' attentions on the aspects that they are about to judge.

- Task. Many subjective concepts are controversial because there are many different interpretations. By segmenting the factors that lead to the subjective decision, it is possible to narrow down the decision space. In our experience, we found that most of the problems occur on ill-defined questions that produce inconsistent answers.

While we may think that HIDDENs waste work, it can be beneficial to test internal features. In our example, Q2 can be used to evaluate the precision or a named-entity extractor component for detecting the type person.

Once we know that the HIT can be carried out by workers, the focus should be on workers' performance to make sure we obtain the best results possible.

3.7   SUMMARY

Quality assessment is key to make sure we get the right labels. It is expected that we need to enforce a high standard and therefore implement the appropriate measures. Depending on the platform, there is the possibility that some built-in quality control mechanisms are available but, in practice, we should not anticipate anything very special.

At the end of the day, as requesters, we should focus on data, qualifying workers, assessing work, and HIT debugging. Poorly designed tasks may be at the root of bad results, rather than worker malice.

We do recommend using inter-rater agreement metrics except percentage agreement but do not expect high values for κ or Krippendorff's α. In the case of information retrieval-related tasks like relevance assessment, the nature of such a multi-dimensional concept and subjectivity do play a role in the difficulty to get high agreement. Instead, we recommend looking at the data and observing patterns in those disagreements. Contingency tables are an excellent complementary tool for analyzing such cases.

"Plus, we double the accuracy at no extra cost by using our extensive pool of Siamese twins."

Pointers

The book by Rosenthal and Rosnow [212] provides comprehensive material on methods and data analysis for behavioral research.

Lease explores other important aspects like data quality control and implications in machine learning and hybrid systems [154]. A framework for estimating worker agreement in crowdsourcing is presented in Checco et al. [47].

CHAPTER 4

Algorithms and Techniques for Quality Control

> The truth may be stretched thin, but it
> never breaks, and it always surfaces above
> lies, as oil floats on water.
>
> Don Quixote

In this chapter we present an overview of the main algorithms for managing quality including the use of worker behavioral data. We also discuss a variety of pragmatic issues that have to do with implementation and scalability.

4.1 FRAMEWORK

Quality control algorithms are a hot topic in crowdsourcing and human computation research and due to the sheer volume of related work, a concise survey and comparison of the many proposed techniques is out of the scope of this chapter.

Instead, we organize the different techniques around two axes: implementation sophistication or complexity and the level of data access for a requester in a given platform. There are some techniques, like majority voting, that are very easy to implement and do not require extra information from the platform. Others, like adaptive algorithms, are more complex and do need worker history, which is only available for platform owners or require a requester to run the same tasks over a longer period of time to obtain such data.

With a practical mindset we group techniques and try to provide a balanced view so requesters can ultimately judge their utility in the context of the application at hand. A HIT that involves categorical answers requires a different quality control mechanism than an annotation task that needs input text from workers. At the end of the day, there are many factors that may influence a requester on selecting which specific technique is more suitable for a given scenario. Examples of such factors are implementation cost, allocated budget, turnaround time, infrastructure required, access to specific platform data, worker history, and behavioral data.

It is also important to identify which labeling task we need to implement. We define a subjective labeling task to be one where the judgment process strongly depends on characteristics of the judge, whereas an objective labeling task is one where judgments solely depend on the document characteristics. We define a partially objective task to be one where there is a best answer. Table 4.1 shows the types of labeling efforts that have been described in the literature.

Table 4.1: A spectrum of labeling tasks, from objective to subjective

Nature of Task	Aggregation Approach	Evaluation Technique
Objective question has a correct answer (objective). For example, is there a cat in this image?	Reliable judge assigns appropriate label for an item.	Evaluate workers by comparing individual results with gold set.
Judgment question has a best answer (partially objective). For example, is this document relevant for this topic?	Inter-rater agreement determines label for an item.	Evaluate workers by comparing individual results with consensus.
Subjective question has consistent answer (subjective). For example, is this tweet interesting for a wider audience?	Repeatable polling determines probability of a label for an item.	Evaluate workers by computing the consistency of results between groups.

4.2   VOTING

Redundancy is one of the oldest tricks in computer science. During the first days of computing, programmers would run the same program twice in a computer and check if the answers were the same as a mechanism for correctness. Fast forward to the current century and majority vote, another form of redundancy, is one of the most common quality control techniques used in practice. We present an overview of the fundamentals of voting.

The simplest and most common procedure for deciding an election between two candidates is the *plurality method*. Each voter cast a vote and the winner is the candidate that receives the most votes. The winner does not need to have a majority of votes. Other methods involve using the rules below that determine the collective outcome by checking whether the number of voters (workers in our case) accepting a preference label l exceeds a threshold. If that is the case, the label l, $l \in L$, set of labels, is collectively accepted.

- Majority. Label l is collectively accepted if there is a majority of workers accepting it: $f_m = \{l >= \lceil (N + 1)/2 \rceil \}$.
- Unanimity. Label l is collectively accepted if all workers accept it: $f_u = \{l >= N\}$.
- Quota. Label l is collectively accepted if there are at least t_l workers that accept it: $f_t = \{l >= t_l\}$.

If there are two candidates, the plurality method is a good choice. However, there are problems when there are more than two candidates. Jean Charles de Borda in the 18th-century showed that plurality may elect the wrong candidate because the method ignores individual preferences over candidates and proposed a new method based on preferences. The Borda count is a method of combining ranking of many individual votes that works as follows. If there are n candidates, each top candidate gets n points, each top place candidate at the second place gets $n - 1$ votes, and so on until the last candidate gets 1 point. The Borda count earned by a candidate j is the sum of rankings assigned by votes, $\sum_{i=1}^{n} v_{ij}$ and the candidate with the largest point total is the winner.

The Marquis du Condorcet proposed a method that selects the candidate that defeats every other candidate in a pair-wise comparison. That is, a candidate who is the winner of a head-to-head comparison with every other candidate.

In practice for tasks that require binary choice answers, majority voting tends to work well using an odd number of workers usually 5 or 7. If there are more choices, the recommendation is to use Borda or Condorcet criterion.

4.3 ATTENTION MONITORING

Due to the repetitive nature of lots of tasks, there is a possibility that workers may miss, unintentionally, certain items. One way to make sure that workers are paying attention is to include checks to monitor concentration, similar to variations of the CAPTCHA technique.

One of the first reports of the use of verifiable answers is the work by Kittur et al. [134] on testing the utility of Mechanical Turk as a platform for conducting user studies. Examples would be to ask a worker what is the title of a web page or how many images are on the document that is being assessed. In other words, make the task difficult to workers who are interested in cheating only. The authors recommend to design HITs such that an accurate completion "requires as much or less effort than non-obvious random or malicious completion".

A variation called Kapcha that forces a slow down in responses is presented in [120]. The Kapcha method involves fading-in the question text and there is evidence that has the potential to reduce satisficing in online surveys. Hauser and Schwarz [97] study instruction manipulation checks (IMC) in surveys and report that Mechanical Turk workers are more attentive to instructions than undergraduate students. Elmalech et al. [75] propose the use of dummy events at different times through the task as an effective mechanism for increasing attention in workers.

4.4 HONEY POTS

One strategy to ensure quality of work is to include, at random, predefined gold standard data in the data set and test workers' performance. The requester interleaves assignments in which the correct answer is already known so it is easy to detect workers who are randomly selecting the answers. This technique also known as "gold data, honey pots, or verifiable answers" is considered an effective solution in practice that produces good results quickly. Tasks are completed faster and we can identify workers who perform poorly very quickly. Workers who tend to fail on the honey pots are usually discarded and marked as not suitable for the task.

While the mechanism is simple, there are some caveats with respect to implementation for an effective execution of this technique at scale. There is an initial cost for producing a known answer that usually involves a domain expert. Then, we need to consider that a percentage of work is spent reproducing answers that we already know. Having workers answer more honey pots helps estimate their performance but leaves less room to work on the unknown items. Using a small number of control checks may not be enough for estimating worker performance.

Gold sets need to be maintained to avoid workers spotting the honey pots and therefore require a process for refreshing data in cases where tasks run daily. Finally, workers are very sensitive to rejections and will contact the requester if they believe the decision was unfair. The requester then has to follow-up with each rejection and this can take a considerable amount of time. Rejecting a large number of answers can get very expensive so it is always a good practice to test and debug the HIT to avoid this kind of situations. In Section 5.5, we show real examples of workers' feedback after a rejection.

Le et al. [153] study the effects of training question distribution in a relevance evaluation task. The gold data is implemented in a dynamic training environment where workers are tested before proceeding to the questions. The authors report that the choice of training examples will affect worker output and recommend the use of a uniform distribution of labels across training data for good results.

The above technique requires a manually generated data set of gold data. In most cases, gold data is generated manually, typically by hired domain experts and the approach is not scalable: it is expensive in terms of cost and time, and error prone. A better solution is to use a small gold set for bootstrapping and then automate the rest.

Oleson et al. [191] propose using the notion of *programmatic gold* for generating gold data automatically that still requires manual intervention but provides savings costs. Programmatic gold is a process of generating gold units with known answers by injecting known types of errors in the dataset. This data manipulation is called pyrite and the first step is identifying worker errors through manual inspection. The second step is to define a set of data transformations that alter certain attributes to produce a new unit that (1) differs from the original violating task requirements and (2) looks like the original. Each data manipulation produces a gold unit that correspond to a particular error. Programmatic gold is a scalable solution for generating gold and it takes the same effort to create 100 or 1,000 gold units.

Abraham et al. [1] describe an algorithm for scalable gold creation using multi-armed bandits. For each worker, combine exploration and exploitation in a single numerical score, updated over time, and at each decision point choose a worker with the highest current score. This score, or index, takes into account both the average skill observed so far (to promote exploitation) and the uncertainty from insufficient sampling (to promote exploration). Over time, the algorithm zooms in on more skilled workers. In a typical application, workers are given a blended stream of new HITs and gold HITs that already belong to the gold HIT set so workers typically do not know if the current HIT is already part of the gold HIT set.

4.5   WORKERS REVIEWING WORK

In this section, we describe human-powered techniques for assessing work quality. More specifically, using workers to self-assess work or to correct and improve previous workers work. At the core, this technique is not new as there are countless examples in the real-world like editors reviewing a story for a newspaper, programmers performing code review, or reviewers reviewing papers for a conference or journal.

These techniques are, in general, easy to implement, provide good results, but may slow down the overall labeling process. This also implies that, as requesters, we may need to implement more than one HIT, which also includes more costs for testing and debugging.

Bernstein et al. [25] introduce the Find-Fix-Verify pattern as a programming solution that splits tasks into three stages.

- Find: Identify patches of work that need more attention.
- Fix. Aggregate answers to find the most consistently reported problem.
- Verify: Perform quality control on revisions.

Find-Fix-Verify is used in Soylent, a word-processing interface that uses the crowd to aid in complex writing tasks. In practice, this pattern is very useful and can be easily adapted to different crowds and platforms.

Hansen et al. [93] compare the effectiveness and efficiency of arbitration and peer review in the context of record transcription. In arbitration, two workers independently transcribe the same item and disagreements go to an arbitrator. In peer review, one worker reviews the other worker's transcription. The authors report that adding a verification step like the one proposed in the Find-Fix-Verify pattern was unnecessary as it increased time but didn't improve quality. Peer-review took less time to complete but in some cases the quality was inferior to arbitration. Experienced workers are more likely to agree than beginners and experts, as expected, take less time to complete work.

Dow et al. [70] study whether task-specific feedback helps workers. The authors found that feedback leads to better work, helps workers learn over time, and motivates more production. They also recommend enumerating concrete criteria for the work output and then ask workers to self reflect on their prior work along those criteria. The study was done in Mechanical Turk writing customer reviews.

A workflow that checks the accuracy of translation quality from Urdu to English by post-editing and ranking is described in Bloodgood and Callison-Burch [27] and Zaidan and Callison-Burch [258]. Techniques for supporting an expert in validating answers provided by workers is presented in Hung et al. [108].

4.6   JUSTIFICATION

In the case of subjective tasks, we can also ask workers to provide a justification or rationale for an answer. A worker who provides a justification is less likely to be a spammer. This way we collect an answer and also the "why" for a response. For IR document relevance assessment tasks, collections like TREC contain labels but no information about why a particular document is relevant or not. By exploiting this technique not only we can capture more signal but we can also use justification as quality control technique.

One way to implement justification is to include an optional open-ended question at the end of the task. Overall, in our experience, less than 30% of the workers provided a justification in our tests HITs. The average comment length varies depending on the task and the incentive. If there is a bonus offered for a comment, then more workers may provide justification. That being said, requesters should not make comments mandatory as workers may not feel like writing meaningful feedback. Our recommendation is to have comments as optional even if a bonus payment is offered. Some examples are as follows:

```
- Highly relevant: focuses on drug routes and mentions the Golden Triangle.
- Some relevance
- Not totally relevant
- About a creative endeavor but not specifically about creativity itself
- Vaguely relevant
- Totally off base
```

A drawback of this approach is that workers need to write down the explanations and a possible explanation is that this extra request makes the HIT more difficult. For requesters, more data processing is needed to parse and categorize the free text that is provided by workers.

McDonnell et al. [181] propose a different avenue by asking workers to copy and paste short document fragments as rationale for supporting their answers. The authors propose a two-stage task where one worker provides the rationale and a second one reviews the work. The authors report that experienced workers provide justifications with no increased cost in time completion. The usability of the HIT in conjunction with dual supervision can be useful for generating gold answers.

MicroTalk is a quality control workflow proposed by Drapeaut et al. [72] that requires workers to justify answers. Initially, the system trains workers on gold standard questions and to get work done, MicroTask uses three primitives to arrive at a consensus answer.

- Assess: Workers are asked to provide an answer to a question.

- Justify: Provide reasoning.

- Reconsider: Workers are presented with an argument for the opposing answer and then asked to confirm or change their answer.

4.7   AGGREGATION METHODS

Other techniques are based on the EM algorithm to estimate workers' accuracy and the final HIT result at the same time [58]. The EM algorithm consists of an Expectation (of missing data) step and a Maximization (maximum likelihood estimation) step:

1. Obtain some initial estimates of the missing data.

2. Calculate the maximum likelihood estimates for the quantities of interest as if the missing data had been found.

3. Now calculate new estimates of the missing data.

4. Repeat steps 2 and 3 until both the maximum likelihood estimates and the missing data estimates converge.

The algorithm updates the estimates for both workers' accuracies and answers until it converges. It computes quality parameters for all workers, considering each instance's current answer (label) as ground truth. It then, computes the most likely label for all instances considering worker's quality parameter as ground truth. The algorithm iterates several times to conversion or for certain number of iterations, and produces the labels. The algorithm assumes that workers who agree with consensus the most on the long run are the most trustworthy.

Sheng et al. [221] introduce the repeated labeling strategy that consists of increasing the number of instances for those answers (labels) that are noisy. This strategy, called "get another label", works well in practice. However, redundancy is not the perfect solution because it may increase the cost of crowdsourcing, thus making it comparable to hired editors. The work presented in Ipeirotis et al. [112] is another algorithm based on EM, with several improvements. EM-based solutions use information from all the HITs in the data set and assume that a worker is answering many (or all) of these HITs and with more or less similar performance across them. However, empirical evidence shows that HITs have widely varying difficulty levels.

Adopting the EM method, Raykar et al. [207] model label expertise. Similarly, Hosseini et al. [102] apply EM to simultaneously predict worker's reliability and the true relevance label for digitized book pages. Whitehill et al. [251] follow a similar approach where worker accuracies are not known a priori. Smyth et al. [224] describe the application of EM for inferring image ground truth in large-scale data set.

Another algorithm, Vox Populi, uses the aggregate label as an approximate ground truth and eliminates the workers that provide incorrect answers [59]. Vox Populi is a data cleaning algorithm that prunes low-quality workers with the goal of improving a training set. The technique uses the aggregate label as an approximate ground truth and eliminates the workers that tend to provide incorrect answers. Karger et al. [122] optimize task allocation given budgets assuming known Bayesian prior on both tasks and judges.

Very recently there are new directions that use adaptive approaches for managing crowds based on explore-exploit tradeoffs. The work by Abraham et al. [1] investigates an adaptive approach in which the crowdsourcing platform adaptively decides how many workers to use before stopping and choosing the answer. An important part is then the design of a stopping rule, that is, an algorithm that at each round decides whether to stop or to ask one more worker. Parameswaran et al. [198] consider a setting similar to the stopping rules presented in Abraham [1] for HITs with two possible answers. They assume that all HITs have the same difficulty level, and that the (two-sided) error probabilities are known to the algorithm.

"Unfortunately, 100% of our teenage
evaluators responded with 'whatever'."

4.8 BEHAVIORAL DATA

A completely different alternative proposed by Rzeszotarski and Kittur [214] is to focus on the way workers work instead of what they produce. That is, capturing and understanding behavioral traces and use these signals to predict quality and task performance. The technique called *task fingerprinting* is about describing the behavior of the workers for a given task. This can be implemented using Javascript to capture user clicks, keystrokes, mouse movements, scrolls, and similar events.

The Wernicke system for collecting information extraction annotations uses many behavioral features and a majority voting algorithm for quality control [92]. The authors show that there is a high correlation between behavioral features and work quality and, in some reported experiments, behavioral features outperform performance-based methods like EM.

Qiu et al [204] propose CrowdSelect, a task assignment strategy that takes into account workers' behavior over tasks. The model consists of two main components: worker error rate prediction and worker selection, and it was tested on a tweet data set labeling task in Mechanical Turk.

4.9   EXPERTISE AND ROUTING

Expert finding is the task to find persons with specific knowledge: "Who are experts on topic X?". Alternatively, instead of finding experts on a specific topic, expert profiling is about finding out which topics a specific person is an expert in. In other words: "What topics does person Y know about?".

If we can capture such information and there is access to historical data, it is possible to employ expertise routing solutions. In several cases, the problem is that workers may not have the expertise required to perform the task so instead of collecting low-quality data, the effort is on proactively routing the task to experts. The ability to manage workers with different levels of expertise and to mix different pools of workers based on different profiles can really help in task assignment. If we assume that there is variance in terms of expertise and knowledge, wouldn't it be better to route work to more prepared workers who would provide better answers? This line of work is still on a very early stage. We describe a number of techniques that are proposed in the literature.

The research by Hassan et al. [234] showed that expertise profiling of workers through self-assessment is beneficial for simple routing tasks. Organisciak et al. [192] propose the idea of personalized crowdsourcing for more subjective tasks and propose two protocols: taste-matching and taste-grokking. Taste-matching recruits workers based on their similarity to the requester and taste-grokking rely on workers predicting the requester's taste or profile. Results show that taste-matching is more effective in complex tasks where grokking works best when there is a small number of workers.

Li et al. [157] propose a crowd targeting framework that can discover if a specific group of workers have a higher quality on a given task. The main idea is to send part of the task to the crowd, analyze the results and find the right group, and use the just discovered group to complete the task.

4.10   SUMMARY

There is a wide range of algorithms to chose from for managing work quality and selecting the appropriate one depends on the application domain, implementation complexity, and the level of data access that we can get from a platform. What we have presented can be viewed as a progression from simple procedures that require basic information to more system-based approaches that use a combination of techniques for managing quality. In practice, other factors like allocated budget for labeling or speed for producing the data may influence our selection, so having a good understanding of the advantages and disadvantages of each algorithm can be very useful in making a decision.

Algorithms running on a machine are easy to replicate. We just code it up in a programming language or use a different data set and we expect equivalent results. Things get more complicated as platforms may have different demographics or features, making the reproducibility a bit trickier. Certain algorithms may have dependencies like work history or reputation, which are difficult to recreate on a platform.

For tasks that require workers to answer by selecting categories from a set of choices, we recommend using an incremental approach starting with majority vote and then evolve into more sophisticated solutions. If the requester has access to platform data like worker history or any other past performance, techniques that require such data may perform better. Using workers to verify other workers' work is a good solution for cases where there is an annotation task or more input data is needed from workers.

Is it better to spend money asking a worker to relabel an existing example or to label a new example? This question is very common in practice and Lin et al. [163] identify three dimensions surrounding the choice of relabeling: (1) the bias of the learning algorithm, (2 the accuracy of workers, and (3) the allocated budget.

Rejecting work can create attrition problems and hurt the requester reputation (see feedback analysis in Section 5.5). A possible solution for borderline workers (not obvious robots) would be to pay the minimum and exclude them in future work within the specific task in question. An item that we have not addressed so far is monetary incentives (see Section 5.3). If we pay more, wouldn't that increase the quality of the work?

Faltings et al. [77] point out that increasing the number of workers is not an effective mechanism for eliminating bias in the case of subjective tasks and suggest bonus schemes as a mechanism to eliminate bias. The rationale is that it is desired to motivate workers to provide unbiased answers to begin with.

A growing number of researchers use crowdsourcing for evaluation, but they do not provide enough details about how their experiments and tasks were conducted. This lack of details makes it impossible to assess the quality of the results. HITs, like any experiment, must be repeatable.

Pointers

Many different quality control algorithms have been proposed in the literature but there is little information on comparisons among them using real-world tasks and data sets. Sheshadri and Lease [222] describe SQUARE, a benchmarking framework for contrasting consensus techniques that includes tasks, data sets, and metrics. Zhang et al. [260] survey techniques and algorithms for ground truth inference and learning models. Wang et al. [247] also survey different algorithms and develop a scheme for binary labeling tasks in a cost-effective manner. Chittilappilly et al. [53] provide an overview of general-purpose crowdsourcing techniques.

Ground truth creation is a problem for new evaluation campaigns when no gold standard is available. Blanco et al. [26] rely on manual creation of gold answers for monitoring worker quality in a semantic search task and show the repeatability of crowdsourcing. Scholer et al. [218] study the feasibility of using duplicate documents as ground truth in test collections. Qiang et al. [167] propose two types of consensus methods that incorporate honey pots: two-stage estimator and joint estimator. Administering language pretests as gold standards for language translations HITs is recommended by Pavlick et al. [202]. Gold judge behavior is studied in Kazai and Zitouni [130].

An introduction to judgment aggregation is presented in Grossi and Pigozzi [90]. Preference voting used by Callison-Burch [40]. Beyond multiple-choice is researched by Lin et al. [162].

Active learning, a technique that reduces the number of required labels has been a choice in a number of applications. Bloodgood and Callison-Burch research active learning with large machine translation data sets [27]. Laws et al. [152] experiment with named-entity extraction and sentiment analysis and recommend the use of active learning and crowdsourcing for the creation of training sets. Other related work on active learning is presented by Bansal et al. [16], Brew et al. [34], Hsueh et al. [106], and Mozafari et al. [185].

Finally, we enumerate research on algorithms, techniques, and related aspects. Budget constraints (Li et al. [158], Chen et al. [48]), worker's accuracy, expertise and reputation (Burnham and Sami [39], Donmez et al. [69], Kumar and Lease [143], Welinder and Perona [250], Raykar et al. [207], Whitehill et al. [251], Kasneci et al. [123], Feng et al. [68], Whiting et al. [252]), task assignment (Ho et al. [98]), mislabel data (Brodley and Friedl [35]), crowd wisdom (Welinder et al. [249], Bachrach et al. [15], Raykar et al. [208], Gadiraju [81], Hata et al. [96]), scalability (Deng et al. [63]), incentives (Hsieh and Kocielnik [105]), adversarial workers (Gadiraju et al. [82], Kurve et al. [144], Vuurens et al. [244]), bias (Wauthier and Jordan [248], Kamar et al. [119]), methodologies (CrowdSynth [117]), processes ([141, 233], Sprouse [228]), and task design (Huang et al. [107], Organisciak and Twidale [193]).

CHAPTER 5

The Human Side of Human Computation

> This is the type of AI that I am interested in—what can the human and machine do together, and not in the competition which can arise.
>
> Richard Hamming

In this chapter, we emphasize the human side of human computation. Who are the workers and what will their concerns be? Are there any legal implications when using humans for micro-tasks? We specifically cover issues like incentives, feedback, quality from a worker's perspective, and ways a requester can improve the experience for workers. We also talk about reputation and what goes on in user forums and discussion groups.

"I don't care. I'm not pressing 'relevant'
unless we get better-tasting pellets."

5.1   OVERVIEW

Crowdsourcing is perceived as a cheaper, faster, and convenient mechanism for recruiting participants. Online experiments are comparable to laboratory and field experiments while requiring less infrastructure and cost to implement. There have been several studies on the benefits of using crowd workers for behavioral science, user studies, and sociology to name a few [22, 38, 45, 101]. The recent book by Gray and Suri [87] covers the many characteristics of "ghost work" and "ghost economy." Instead of reviewing and contrasting all existing work, we take, one more time, a practical view and group workers' characteristics in to the following categories:

- Demographics: Who are the workers?
- Incentives: Why do people work and what are the incentives?
- Experience: How is life as a worker in a crowdsourcing platform?
- Feedback: What is their feedback for requesters and as users of such platforms?
- Legal and ethics: What do we need to know as workers and requesters?

We are interested in the above categories as requirements for designing good HITs that can be completed on time and that workers can feel comfortable working on.

5.2   DEMOGRAPHICS

A number of demographic studies have been performed in Mechanical Turk. Ipeirotis conducted one of the first surveys and reported that approximately 50% of the workers come from the U.S. and 40% come from India, and that monetary incentive is the primary motivation for performing work [110]. In another survey, Paolacci et al. [196] report a breakdown of 47% for the U.S. and 34% for India with respect to workers' country of origin. Ross et al. [213] study the workforce for a period of 20 months and report a more international workforce.

In a more recent work, Ipeirotis made available an online tool called MTurk Tracker[1] that runs continuously surveys of the worker population and displays live statistics like gender, age, income, and country, to name a few. A current breakdown shows that approximately 80% of the Mechanical Turk workers are from the U.S. and 20% are from India.[2]

Difallah et al. [64] analyzed data from Mechanical Turk on a number of dimensions like topic, task type, reward evolution, platform throughput, and supply and demand. The findings indicate that most of HITs require U.S.-based workers and survey-type tasks are the most popular ones. In a follow-up work, Difallah et al. [66] study demographics and dynamics of workers by conducting a survey over a period of 28 months with 85,000 responses from 40,000 unique participants. The authors presented an analysis of population estimation and derive the number of available workers at any given time, which is approximately 2,450 workers. A related marketplace analysis is described in Ipeirotis [109].

---

[1]http://demographics.mturk-tracker.com/#/gender/all
[2]http://www.behind-the-enemy-lines.com/2015/04/demographics-of-mechanical-turk-now.html

Jain et al. [115] conducted an experimental analysis of 27 million microtasks performed by over 70,000 workers that focused on marketplace dynamics, task design, and worker behavior. They observe that tasks with detailed instructions and examples has the effect of decreasing disagreement. In contrast, tasks that require workers to answer a high number of questions show higher disagreement.

There are some issues with running surveys in crowdsourcing platforms as workers may never see the HIT or may not provide answers if the design is cumbersome or payment is low. A novel approach is the methodology proposed by Pavlick et al. [202] for language demographics that relies on creating HITs in 100 languages that require translating 10 foreign words into English. The authors group answers by language, quality, and speed and recommend the following languages that have large populations in Mechanical Turk who complete HITs accurately: Dutch, French, German, Gujarati, Italian, Kannada, Malayalam, Portuguese, Romanian, Serbian, Spanish, Tagalog, and Telegu.

5.3   INCENTIVES

The main incentive for performing work in a crowdsourcing platform is money and workers expect fair payment. There are other reasons that workers may participate like altruism, social good, fun, and killing time, but for the most part, workers expect money for work performed.

The rule of thumb for requesters is to pay federal minimum wage in the U.S. How much money do workers make on crowdsourcing platforms? Hara et al. [94] conducted a data analysis on earnings and estimate that 96% of workers on Mechanical Turk earn below the federal minimum wage. Analysis on data from 2,600 workers performing 3.8 million tasks show a median hourly wage of $2/hr and only 4% of workers earned more that $7.25/hr. There are lower-paying requesters that post lot of work and thus drive down the overall wage distribution. Callison-Burch [41] describe a browser extension for Chrome (`crowd-workers.com`) that allow workers to work more efficiently on Mechanical Turk by discovering high paying work. Results of a pilot study on 110 workers performing 77,000 tasks show that the average hourly earning was $9.56 (median was $7.85).

Berg [23] analyzes survey data on Mechanical Turk and Crowdflower workers and provides an interesting view into the workforce. Workers in general have concerns over pay structure and poor communication with requesters. Berg also reports that 40% of respondents rely on crowdwork as the main source of income.

One of the early works on monetary incentives is the research by Mason and Watts [178] where they found that increased financial incentives increase the quantity, but not the quality of work performed by the workers. They explain the difference as an "anchoring" effect: people who were paid more also perceived the value of their work to be greater, and thus were not more motivated than people who were paid less. Ho et al. [99] conducted many experiments and found that performance payment improves task quality and bonus payment has implications in work results. As long as the bonus sum is important, the quality of work improved.

As we can see, incentives are a good mechanism to draw attention from the pool of workers. However, incentives can have an impact regarding who participates. Hsieh et al. [105] study incentives and participation bias, and show evidence that the combination of incentives and participants can result in different task outcomes.

Do workers who volunteer perform at the same level as workers who are looking to make only money? Mao et al. [170] study the performance of volunteers and regular workers in a citizen science scenario. They find that, given the correct incentives, regular workers produce similar quality of work compared to volunteers. In another study, Rogstadius et al. [211] report that workers were more precise when performing work for a non-profit than for a for-profit requester.

5.4   WORKER EXPERIENCE

How is life as a worker in a crowdsourcing platform? Besides job satisfaction and monetary rewards, what other important information can we learn from workers with the goal of improving our tasks?

One of the first studies on how workers search for work is described by Chilton et al. [50] where the authors scrape tasks in Mechanical Turk and conducted a survey among workers. Workers tend to sort HITs by recency and size and mostly look at the tasks in the first two pages of the search results. Kaplan et al. [121] survey work strategies and tools used among workers for finding and completing work. An interesting strategy used by workers is called PandA (Preview and Accept) where workers accept a batch of similar HITs to work through. Another finding is that 30% of respondents reported problems when searching for good HITs. As we said early on, good task description and content are desired features for attracting workers.

Brawley and Pury [33] investigate worker job satisfaction, information sharing, and turnover by running HITs for U.S. and India residents on Mechanical Turk and suggest that "intrinsic motivation is a stronger predict of job satisfaction." The authors report that the top positive requesters' behaviors resulting in the highest job satisfaction ratings were: building an ongoing relationship with workers, providing encouraging feedback; posting simple HITs that paid well; posting HITs that were interesting; and proving a progress bar. The negative requester behaviors resulting in the lowest ratings: paying an unfair wage; including difficult attention check questions; using majority rules for rejection decisions; advertising a HIT as taking less time that it actually does; and blaming others.

Marshall and Shipman [175] describe the results of 6 studies using open-ended questions and structured statements with a worker population of around 1,200 participants on Mechanical Turk. This research was focused on more "survey-style" work and an interesting finding is that "workers exhibit a capacity for completing long surveys as long as they are engaged and their efforts are respected." Similar to what is reported in [178], the authors comment that if monetary incentive was the key, workers would have not written long answers in the open-ended questions. An advantage of crowdsourcing for these type of studies is diversity. Consistent findings with similar research is that work is not always done in isolation and good design coupled with interesting content are good requisites for high-quality data.

In a study conducted in Mechanical Turk, Antin and Shaw [12] note that online motivation can be subject to social desirability bias, the tendency to respond in ways that participants believe would appear desirable to others, and suggest that surveys with sensitive topics could reflect this bias in the results.

Martin et al. [176] conduct an ethnomethodological analysis of publicly available content on Turker Nation instead of a survey or HIT. Consistent with other studies, the authors report that monetary incentive is an important factor for workers as they view platforms as a labor marketplace. Having enough information on good and bad requesters and HIT descriptions is part of workers' decision making for selecting tasks to work on. Workers are offended when requesters reject HITs with unclear explanations and don't like blocking (banning a worker from working on a HIT).

There is recent research that shows that the crowd is not a group of independent workers and that workers communicate and collaborate with each other [88, 175, 176, 217]. Gray et al. [88] describe three main types of collaboration: (1) administrative overhead, (2) notification of high quality HITs; and (3) helping each other with work on HITs. Ying et al. [257] design and implement a HIT in which 10,000 workers self report their communication links to other workers in Mechanical Turk. This communication network within the crowd has implications for requesters as workers may not be an independent sample.

Another perspective is the work by Schmidt [217] where he reports his experience first hand as a worker in Mechanical Turk over 50 days working on 806 HITs. Schmidt also reports that workers are not autonomous individuals and highlights the importance of the communities that exist around Mechanical Turk.

Finally, there are communities around specific platforms like Turker Nation[3] and MTurk Forum[4] where workers share information about tasks and requesters. Most of these sites would have work providers hall of fame/shame information which is used by workers to find good requesters and avoid bad ones. Irani and Silberman present Turkopticon, a browser extension that augments workers' view of HITs with information about requesters by providing support for evaluating work requests [113]. We should not underestimate the importance of workers discussing about our work. The famous Cambridge Analytica fiasco is such an example.[5]

---

[3]http://turkernation.com/

[4]http://mturkforum.com/

[5]https://www.technologyreview.com/the-download/610598/the-scientist-who-gave-cambridge-analytica-its-facebook-data-got-lousy-reviews/

5.5   WORKER FEEDBACK

Workers can provide feedback in HITs, if there is an open-ended input text available, by communicating directly with requesters within the platform, or by sharing information in the many forums and online communities.

5.5.1   OPERATIONAL

Operational feedback involves workers mentioning issues with the live HIT. Examples are comments about a particular missing item, errors, or unclear instructions with respect to special cases. As anecdotal evidence, if one of the tasks we had a broken link and a number of workers mentioned that the website was loading while one marked as "relevant." The latter was obviously a spammer or robot so we decided to keep it as a sanity check that workers are paying attention to the task.

5.5.2   GENERAL COMMUNICATION

Feedback about general communication between worker and requester is usually about a positive or negative experience working on the HIT. Below, we present, verbatim, samples of exchanges with workers.

As expected, there is more communication when work is rejected.

```
Worker X1: I did. If you read these articles most of them have nothing to
do with space programs. I'm not an idiot.
```

```
Worker X2: As far as I remember there wasn't an explanation about what
to do when there is no name in the text. I believe I did write a few
comments on that, too. So I think you're being unfair rejecting my HITs.
```

Positive feedback:

```
Worker X3: Thank you. I will post positive feedback for you at Turker
Nation.
Author: was this a sarcastic comment?
Worker X3: I took a chance by accepting some of your HITs to see if you
were a trustworthy author. My experience with you has been favorable
so I will put in a good word for you on that website.  This will help you
get higher quality applicants in the future, which will provide higher
quality work, which might be worth more to you, which hopefully
means higher HIT amounts in the future.
```

5.5.3   HIT ASSESSMENT

In some cases, workers may find that a particular topic or data set requires more expertise to correctly answer. We can explicitly ask workers if the HIT is difficult. For example, we can extend the relevance template from Section 2.11.1, and ask workers to rate the difficulty of the topic on a scale 1–5 (1=easy, 5=very difficult)

Figure 5.1 shows topics sorted by the average rating by workers (five workers per assignment). The x-axis shows the topic labels and the y-axis shows the difficulty scale. We can see that for topics like airport security, inventions, and tourism workers found the topic easy. Other themes like Greek, philosophy, and foreign minorities usually require more background so it is expected to see the increase on perceived difficulty of the topic. This information can be used to assign weight to the relevance scores if the workers are more or less confident with the respect to a particular topic.

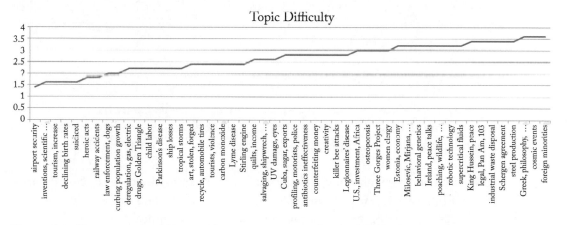

Figure 5.1: Topics arranged by workers in increasing level of difficulty.

5.6   LEGAL AND ETHICS

There is agreement in published research that workers are closer to the U.S. population as a whole than subjects recruited from traditional university subject pools. There are, however, ethical issues when conducting online research that we need to be familiar with like informed consent, right to withdraw, confidentiality, and copyrighted materials. In crowdsourcing practice, there is very little information on how to manage these items and we refer to existing work from psychological research for advice [18].

Felstiner [78] uses Mechanical Turk as a case study for investigating employment relationship and labor law in crowdsourcing. Wolfson and Lease [254] examine the following legal issues that requesters and platform providers should be aware of when implementing crowdsourcing:

employment law, patent inventorship, data security, copyright ownership, and securities regulation with respect to crowdfunding. The authors provide the following recommendations.

- Be mindful of the law.
- Use contracts to clearly define the relationship between employer and worker.
- Be open and honest about expectations, work offered, and how you will use the data collected.

Harris [95] studies tasks that are not illegal but can be considered unethical and describe common techniques that can be found in such tasks like social engineering, human computation tests, and attack and run. Examples of such tasks are review manipulation and information gathering through misrepresentation. Harris observes that many workers may be unaware that the task they are performing is unethical.

The study by Matin et al. [176] examines examples from Turker Nation where workers complain about being categorized as spammers or bots for reasons they do not understand, which has an effect of on workers' approval rating.

5.7 SUMMARY

Most studies on demographics, worker experience, and worker feedback are based on research conducted on Mechanical Turk. While this is a good initial step in understanding crowd dynamics in crowdsourcing, there are other platforms (internal and external) where little information is known.

For workers, a good compensation is the primary consideration followed by task duration and number of HITs available. As a requester, our goal is to design and implement tasks that produce the right results, and, at the same time, these tasks have to appeal to workers. We want qualified workers and honest answers for the work that we provide. Managing a pool of workers and tasks is a daily activity and it could be more difficult than managing computers. Worker attrition is a problem as without human power, HITs are not going to get done. Maintaining a positive reputation among workers is key for long-term projects. Workers trust the requester when payment is fair and on time, and there is a clear explanation if there is a rejection.

Finally, we provided a high-level overview of the legal issues when collecting data via crowdsourcing and tasks that may be unethical.

Pointers

The book by Gray and Suri [87] provides an in-depth description of the invisible human workforce that helps improve many systems by performing micro-work. Irani and Silberman continue their work on Turkopticon and present a perspective on labor, ethics, and design in [114]. Kamar and Horvitz [118] introduce the consensus predict rule that rewards a worker based on how well his/her report can predict consensus.

CHAPTER 6

Putting All Things Together

> Hence, plan to throw one away; you will,
> anyhow.
>
> ———————————————————————
>
> Fred Brooks Jr.

In this chapter, we take a programming view and present a perspective for programming tasks that requires a combination of humans and machines. We draw parallels to software engineering practices that boost program quality, where they should be adopted, and where they are insufficient for this novel domain. We focus on five main topics: programming crowds, testing and debugging tasks, quality control, managing the development process, and operational items.

6.1   THE STATE OF THE PRACTICE

The requirements from customers are very clear: high throughput with good quality at a manageable cost. The reality in the field is more complex and involves a delicate balance among those specifications that also depend on specific cases. A typical solution is to design a data-processing workflow that optimizes accuracy, processing speed, and cost.

There is little published literature on shared practices about development methodologies and processes in projects that involve large-scale labeling or systems that require humans and machines working in synchronization. The book by Marcus and Parameswaran [171] provides a review of the main techniques and outlines problems encountered in the field. The authors surveyed industry users and marketplace providers and present a good perspective on crowdsourcing with respect to data management, usage, and cost. We would like to highlight a couple of items from the survey of industry users: (1) classification and entity resolution tasks are very popular and (2) most solutions include simple work quality control schemes.

So far in this book we have covered many aspects related to human computation and it should be clear by now that human computation-based applications are a new avenue for using resources of today's digitally connected, global workforce. However, there are some practical issues with the adoption of human computation and crowdsourcing at scale in organizations. Crowdsourcing works but requires a solid software construction approach along with the usage of data management principles. Researchers and practitioners need to be responsible for acquiring the best possible labels and should own the entire process. In other words, the work is outsourced to the crowd but not the engineering process.

All crowd-based computation is performed usually by running dedicated tasks in a commercial platform or a home-grown system, which is the case for large companies. Some organizations use a hybrid model that combines crowdsourcing in the wild with a third-party vendor that provides editorial support.

While it is true that current platforms offer very limited functionality, we argue that most of the problems in practice stem from poor engineering skills.

6.2   WETWARE PROGRAMMING

Programmers know that by coding precise instructions on a language, machines do exactly as they are told. When humans execute code, the story is different: the instruction set for humans is somewhat unknown, making it more difficult for an engineer to design and implement solutions based on human computation.

There are well-known techniques for avoiding writing bad programs [131] and a good awareness of the construction aspect as a central activity in modern software engineering [179]. Unfortunately, this is not the case with the nascent human computation field. We claim that practitioners need to use proven programming principles as much as possible, while at the same time taking into consideration the human aspects of human computation. We expect new techniques, programming languages, and design patterns to be devised in the near future. This is exactly why crowd-based computing at scale is an exciting area.

6.2.1   WHAT TO MEASURE

We need to be able to trust the data collected so far. A way to achieve this is to use statistics that can help measure reliability and agreement. Because we will be collecting data and labels many times, we need to be able to know if the measures are consistent over time. With computers, we know that the program will execute and produce expected results in different machines assuming they have similar characteristics. With humans, that assumption is not always true. If we execute the same HIT on different days, different workers would work on it and variability in the results is expected.

6.2.2   PROGRAM STRUCTURE AND DESIGN PATTERNS

In software engineering, Conway's law states that the system architecture will reflect the communication structure of the team that built them. A similar phenomenon at the design phase is visible for ML-based applications: the structure of a HIT mirrors the structure of the task that the developer is working on. If the engineering task is to build, say, a web query classifier, then the engineer designs a HIT so humans can categorize a query and use such data as input to a specific modeling tool. This design approach looks fine as a data collection technique but has the effect of creating monolithic HITs that do too much and can be inherently complex. While this may work for small and very specific cases, it does not for others.

If the HIT requires improvement, asking another question or including a few more examples to the instructions is a common practice. However, the HIT complexity increases and even instructions that used to be very simple at the beginning can blow up to be several pages. This creates frustration with workers and developers. Can we do better?

In general, there are two ways to succeed at implementing HITs at scale. The first, is to think of a HIT like any other piece of software and use established programming practices. The second, is to use the same techniques carefully as they are proven to work with machines, but they may not be suitable for humans.

The type and characteristics of labels that are needed for the machine may not be applicable for humans. That is, as task designers, we need to find ways to ask workers to perform a task that they are comfortable working with instead of forcing them to use the labeling strategy that we need. The example presented in Section 3.6 shows a detailed case trying to find categories for workers.

In practice, not all tasks are simple to implement and a common mistake is trying to do too much on a single HIT. That is, asking several questions while minimizing payment instead of a more practical alternative of decomposing a task into smaller ones. At first, refactoring a HIT looks counter intuitive: we pay more, there is more engineering work, and it looks like it would take longer to collect the results.

The fact that we would like to get the best label possible does not mean that such a label needs to be produced in a single task in one pass. Lessons learned from software design tell us that partitioning a problem into small pieces is a good thing. Smaller HITs are easier to debug, an already very hard problem that we described in Section 3.6. A good HIT can be reused by other teams or for another similar workflow. HITs that are easier to debug, easier to maintain, and easier to share are, in general, more reliable. By using modularization techniques, we end up paying only for the work that is needed and it is also possibly to parallelize some HITs, which speeds up the entire process.

We need to design HITs that humans can do well and, if possible, to think in terms of data pipelines and workflows, and quite possibly the combination of humans and machines if needed. A number of design patterns have been proposed in the literature like find-fix-verify, iterative refinement, do-verify, and partition-map-reduce to name a few.

6.2.3 DEVELOPMENT PROCESS

Engineers in an organization use a specific development process to produce software. However, when dealing with a human instruction set, the process is ad hoc at best. It is good practice to have a development process in place that enables fast HIT prototyping and experimentation.

We introduce a simple methodology for designing and implementing HITs in the context of two conditions that can be found in an industrial setting: *continuity* and *scalability*. By continuity, we mean continuous execution of tasks. That is, running repeatable tasks over longer periods of time like relevance evaluation. Scalability is about the capacity to process large quantities of data.

The proposed method is independent of the crowdsourcing platform of choice, workforce, and task type. At a very high level, we describe a sequence of actions over time that can be seen as an incremental series of steps for running tasks, as presented in Figure 6.1. Early stages of the method emphasize coding and design; later stages focus more closely on work quality. This proposed scheme is also applicable to internal systems and for-hire editors. We now describe each part in more detail.

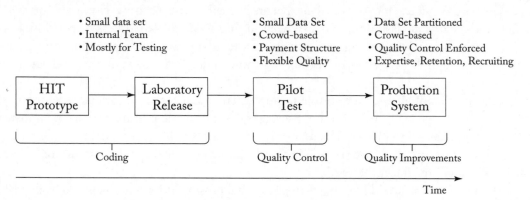

Figure 6.1: Methodology for designing and implementing HITs. Three main phases: (1) coding using well-known programming practices with placeholders for quality and payment; (2) initial quality control with redundancy and payment structure; and (3) quality control improvements by adding human layer (expertise, retention, recruiting).

Laboratory Prototype

Start with a small data set and use it with our very own development team for testing the designs and gathering results. If the design is not clear or if the inter-rater agreement among the development team is low, we need to go back to the drawing board.

If we are not familiar with a particular crowdsourcing platform, the very first step is to select a service, sign up, and do some work for a period of time. The goal here is for the developer or requester to get an idea of the kind of tasks that are available and to experience what an average worker has to do to complete work and get paid. As a worker, we can observe a number of things: some tasks do not require a lot of knowledge or training; some are ill-defined; the pay is low for the workload; the allocated time to complete the task is not sufficient; and so on. These are important considerations that can shape the overall result of a task or experiment, so it is important to do work for other requesters and take note of issues encountered. Familiarity with availability functionality and hands-on experience can give the designer a good overview on what to expect from future workers and how to design the HIT.

The next step is to select a task like document relevance assessment or image labeling and prepare a small data set. The data set preparation is straightforward: choose a subset of a document collection like TREC or Wikipedia, select a few topics, and, for each topic, select also a few documents. For the task, we can start with a high-level goal like "we would like to assess if a document if relevant to a given topic" and then describe the question(s) and flow in more detail. We can think of this step as the *task specification*.

Next, we need to implement the task specification in the task *description language* of the selected crowdsourcing platform. Usually all platforms provide a web form-like mechanism to create tasks, so all that is needed is to take the specification document and create the appropriate version. Similar to traditional software development, the task designer implements the task and tests the functionality using a sample data set. An English major in charge on writing the instructions is much preferred to engineers.

Once the task is ready, it is time to engage with the first type of crowd: our very own internal team. The goal of this step is to test and debug the HIT with experts that know the area very well. Our team performs the work and the HIT designer takes notes about things that are working and which parts of the HIT are difficult. For example, layout issues, the respondent has problem understanding object (e.g., instructions, task, examples, question), the respondent has trouble providing answer to question, and other problems. This exercise is very important so it is desirable that all members of the team provide suggestions and improvements to the entire experience.

Following the completion of the test case, we compute inter-rater agreement among the internal team and go over the feedback. The designer needs to revise questions that cause difficulty and fix all other issues. If the changes are substantial, the same team needs to re-test the experiment to ensure that the new version has improved. This step should yield a higher agreement and consensus that the test satisfies the designer's goals. It is important to note that, like programming, more bugs can appear over time. As we will see later, worker feedback is very useful in identifying issues in the task; therefore, having an optional open-ended questions is usually very valuable.

Pilot Test

This step uses the design that was approved by the team and the same data set as in the previous step but this time using a different crowd: hired editors (if they are available) or crowdsourced workers. The goal is to see if other workers can perform the same task and produce similar results compared to the internal team. If the task design is still unclear and the agreement is low, we probably need to debug the task and repeat.

The main objective if this phase is to test the HIT with a much bigger crowd and use the results for *calibration* purposes and other adjustments. In this phase, there is a payment structure in place and it is unlikely that the results would be useful labels. The overall budget has to include the cost of testing the HIT.

At the beginning, we use the same experiment that was developed in the previous phase with the same data set and involve an external crowd. Typically, we can use a simple set up such as three unique workers per task and a minimum payment as incentive. In this first run, the main goal is to gather data points to answer a few questions: How long does the task take to complete? Do workers understand the instructions? Do the results look as expected? Is there a common theme on the feedback?

One way to measure the performance of both crowds (internal and external) is to compute inter-rater agreement, label distributions, and other metrics that we are interested in. We examine the results by hand and look for outliers, performing an error analysis to identify cases in which the answers are wrong. In many cases, the problem is not that the workers are wrong, but rather that there are problems with the task itself. As in the previous step, the instructions may not be clear or the examples are not be representative.

Small changes may impact the understanding of the task, so having a technical writer review the instructions and examples is usually a good idea in this stage. Those items should be easy to fix and confirm through another run. If the task requires more effort than anticipated or if workers mention via feedback that the incentive is low, the payment can be increased. The focus on this step is making sure that the HIT can be completed without problems by people that are not experts.

Production

Once the design has been tested a number of times and the results are good with a number of pilot tests, the next step is to enforce more on work quality and increase the size of the data set. The previous two stages were helpful in the design, development, and debugging of the task. Now we are in production mode where the emphasis is on monitoring work quality and unexpected issues, making sure that the tasks get done on time and budget.

Besides tuning work quality items, other things to consider in this stage are the implementation of proper sampling techniques [62, 168] and data partitioning strategies for our data sets.

Are we done? Not really as there is always room for improvements. Once the HIT is in production for some time, we can learn a few more things. By now, we have access to more data about workers and we can use techniques that need worker behavioral data. That is, expertise detection, recruiting new workers, and modifications to any payment structure and other incentives for retaining the existing worker pool. All of these techniques can be used to improve the overall quality of results.

6.3   TESTING AND DEBUGGING

Testing and debugging techniques are well understood in modern software development. In essence, testing is about finding ways to break a program and debugging is about identifying and correcting the cause of the problem. Things are very different in the crowdsourcing world:

testing is usually performed in an ad-hoc manner and if things do not work our way, there is usually an adversarial thinking: the workers are to blame. The rationale is that workers are spammers or a lazy bunch trying to get our money by proving bad work or not work at all.

To make things worse, throwaway prototypes are common when writing programs but not so much with human computation. One possible explanation is that there is money spent in the task (payment to workers) and therefore there is some hesitation to discard the results. Some of those labels might be useful, right? As we are going to see, this is not necessary the case. If the task has a problem, then there is no need to squeeze potential good data (this may be due to chance). Clearly, more work needs to be done for improving debugging. Table 6.1 summarizes the differences with traditional software quality assurance.

Table 6.1: Comparison of machine vs. human computation in the development phases of design, testing, and debugging

Phase	Machine Computation	Human Computation
Design	Throw away prototype	Reluctant to throw away a HIT
Testing	Systematic	Ad hoc
Debugging	Programmer's fault	Worker's fault

When testing a HIT, we should follow the same methodology for code. That is, test input for validity, data problems, and plausibility at the unit level. If the HIT is part of a data pipeline it is important to perform extra testing of data integration and flow. Debugging is a different story due to the difficulty of isolating three main factors: data issues, worker performance, and task design. These factors have an interesting dynamic at run time: (1) the data set used for our crowdsourcing task can be problematic due to sampling or biased issues; (2) the pool of workers performing the task are spammers; and (3) the design is defective making it difficult for anyone to perform the task. The "data-worker-task" debugging pattern described in Alonso et al. [6] is a good framework for debugging issues, as we saw in Chapter 4.

Finally, a couple of handy tips from the testing community that can save us time and effort: (1) change one thing at a time and (2) keep an audit trail of what was done in what order. We can debug a HIT with a few items (e.g., documents, images, etc.) to isolate a particular problem and save time and money.

6.4   WORK QUALITY CONTROL

Work quality control techniques are an active area of research in human computation and crowd-sourcing. In this context, we say that a data set of labels is of good quality when it meets internal customer needs and is free from deficiencies.

There are two main questions when looking at solutions that can produce good outcome: (1) when and how should we enforce quality control and (2) how do we measure work quality? To

"We were wondering when the testing would be done."

address quality issues, we need to look at instrumentation, workflows that can modularize tasks, algorithms, and worker behavioral features. Crowd-based applications involve using humans and humans can produce errors, therefore we rely on redundancy or aggregation algorithms to ensure high quality output.

6.4.1   INSTRUMENTATION

Work quality control is an on-going activity, in particular in industrial environments that require tasks to run continuously for longer periods of time. Instrumentation for enforcing work quality control check points should be placed as follows.

- Before HIT goes in production by internal testing or using a qualification test, routing, or similar mechanism to select or recruit workers.

- During HIT execution time by assessing work as workers produce answers using honey pots as random checks or HIDDENs.

- After HIT has completed by computing accuracy metrics and removing bad performers and/or sub-standard work.

6.4.2   ALGORITHMS

As noted before, honey pots are a good technique for comparing a label to a predefined answer. This is very cheap to implement and efficient at run time, but assumes the existence of a gold set or ground truth, which may be problematic in certain domains. A second problem is the requirement to produce good honey pots that are not so easy to identify by workers and on-going maintenance to minimize repetition.

A number of algorithms for managing work quality are based on a majority vote strategy. Majority vote is straightforward to implement and tends to produce in practice, good results. Other consensus and aggregation rules like unanimity and quota can be used as alternatives.

EM-based algorithms are also a popular choice in the field and the already-mentioned book by Marcus and Parameswaran [171] describes the scenarios in which those algorithms are used in practice. One problem with some of these algorithms is that they assume the existence of workers' historical performance, which may not be practical in certain organizations that rely on external crowdsourcing platforms.

Algorithmic solutions for crowdsourcing are still far from other engineering systems that cope well with reliability problems. In general, practitioners using human computation need to be aware of complexity costs, data input assumptions, and likelihood of worst-case scenarios when deciding which algorithm to implement. The more data access and platform control, the better we can do in terms of quality. In practice, however, this is rarely the case so we should not expect crowdsourcing platforms to provide all quality control mechanisms.

Other options are to compare the performance of a worker to other workers in the same task or to use a tiered approach, where certain workers are more experts than others. An example of a tiered approach is the "find-fix-verify" pattern: one set of workers find and fix a problem and a separate set of workers verify that the correction is good. Another example is to use experts to break ties when there is no consensus with other workers.

There has been new research that proposes to enhance worker performance is by providing micro diversions that provide some relief to workers during long sequences of microtasks. Because a lot of tasks are repetitive and, in certain cases, probably boring, providing workers with a break can potentially improve overall work quality. Research has shown that the use of micro breaks as part of a workflow improves worker retention and answer speed while maintaining work quality [55].

6.4.3 BEHAVIORAL DATA

The more data signals we have in terms of HIT usage and worker activity the better. Such information can be used to create work history, worker past performance, and other indicators. Behavioral information like search query logs, clicks, and mouse data can be very useful for understanding what workers like and even for performing HIT A-B design comparisons. Unfortunately, not all these types of data are available to the average requester. The requester usually have only access to time spent on work items and similar data. The rest of the behavioral data is available to platform owners only.

6.4.4 INCENTIVES

In practice, there is usually an established budget for labeling tasks or the requester has to estimate such budget. Of the budget, we need to break down how much we plan to spend on testing, labeling, and evaluation.

How much should we pay for a HIT? While a requester may want to pay as little as possible, in reality, if the pay is too low the work won't get done. As a requester, doing work as part of testing would reveal how much work the HIT requires and this could be a good estimation for payment. Ensuring minimum wage is a good starting point. Bonus payment for good work as further incentive is also desired. Besides the monetary incentive, workers are motivated to work if the task is fun, interesting, or educational. It makes sense to spend effort on providing high quality content and design tasks that are sleek.

6.4.5   DISCUSSION

Given the importance of quality in crowd-based computing, which techniques should we use? It all depends on what kind of infrastructure access we have and the implementation complexity of the algorithms.

If we own the platform, there is a lot behavioral and historical data that we can use to not only improve quality but also to detect spammers, expertise, usage patterns, etc. If we are just a regular requester, then only a set of features are available from the platform that limit the ability to implement specific solutions. In terms of implementation cost, some algorithms have nice properties but, in practice, they can be complex to program or take longer to produce results compared to much simpler and, at the same time, limited ones.

At first, we need to familiarize with a platform and the specific task at hand so a simple quality control algorithm, say A, would work to get things going. As we get more experienced and adjust things on the HIT, we can try a more complex algorithm, B, that should perform better but requires a bit more information from the platform.

A good strategy for managing the implementation of work quality algorithms is to take an incremental approach and compare against a baseline for improvements. For example, say that our algorithm A works fine but we believe that B can do better. Using A as a baseline, we test the performance of B with a small data set and measure if the changes are worth it. In other cases, we may have different strategies for assessing quality. For example, we could have a majority vote-based implementation for one task that is also used for generating a gold set and a more sophisticated algorithm in a separate task.

Do answer some of the HITs yourself. This will often reveal problems in the task design, such as ambiguous questions or cases that are not covered by the instructions or answers, all important aspects of quality. The solved HITs can also be used as honey pots or part of a gold standard.

We don't want to sound repetitive but we can't emphasize enough the importance of testing HITs before they go in production. A large portion of work quality issues can be reduced by proper testing. In general, voting, honey pots, and peer-review methods do work well so we do recommend using them as initial quality control mechanisms before trying out more sophisticated approaches.

6.5   MANAGING CONSTRUCTION

Common feedback from engineers trying crowd-based solutions is that it involves non-trivial implementation effort. We believe that good standards for data quality and experimental design should be enforced to make sure we get the right output from crowd-based applications. After all, labels will be used for rankers, ML models, evaluations, etc. Hence, it is advised not to cut corners. While this may look like a lot of work, if we approach it from the programming side, things look familiar. There is, however, a noticeable difference: programming machines is hard, but programming applications that involve computations performed by machines and humans is *harder*. Table 6.2 summarizes a number of practical recommendations for each stage of the development cycle.

Table 6.2: Practical recommendations per development phase

Phase	Recommendation
Coding	One programming language for extracting data from computing clusters and compute metrics. Avoid moving data around from different systems using different tools as they may introduce problems with encoding and data formats.
Design	Embrace simplicity and use patterns as much as possible. Examples: iterative refinement, find-fix-verify, do-verify, partition-map-reduce, price-divide-solve. Get ready to throw away HITs and results.
Modularization	Design HITs that humans can do well. Think in terms of pipelines and work-flows.
Testing and debugging	Do not patch a bad HIT: rewrite it. Identify problems with data, workers, and task design. Keep a log of things that do not work.
Maintenance	Version all templates and metadata including payments and incentive structure.
Monitoring	Dashboard and alerts.
Documentation	Document the essence of the HIT and its mechanics/integration points.

In the context of implementing massive mining applications, developers are used to run jobs on large computing clusters where there is infrastructure support for data processing. Managing crowds is also different from managing clusters: humans and their time is a precious resource. A number of operational settings become important, in particular scheduling and monitoring.

We expect that some of the HITs will be running for some period of time and, like any piece of technology, maintenance is inevitable. Software maintenance activities can be categorized as: adaptive, perfective, corrective, and preventive [160]. In the context of crowdsourcing and human computation, we refer to maintenance as any work done to change the HIT after it is in operation and identify as perfective as the most important activity. Perfective maintenance is about adding new requirements, improving quality control mechanisms, and document the new changes.

Finally, reproducibility is another topic that requires focus. It is usually difficult to run HITs again and get the exact same results as workers may change. When trying to replicate results, documentation of tasks and any metadata is very useful. Finally, we need to write HITs that are portable, in terms of task design, to any platform.

6.6 OPERATIONAL CONSIDERATIONS

When to schedule a task is very important if large data sets are involved. In any platform at a given time, there are probably thousands of tasks being executed. When is the best time to schedule a task and how large should it be in terms of data size and duration? Instead of launching a single task with a large data set (e.g., 1M items), it is desirable to partition the data in smaller pieces and upload more frequently.

Monitoring can help identify tasks that take longer than expected or, in a worst case, do not attract workers. Does it mean that we should not try again or is that an indication that this particular task is not suitable for crowdsourcing?

Similar to a web search engine where competing pages try to rank higher on the search results page, we would like to place our task on the first page of the crowdsourcing platform of choice. Initially, we can launch and monitor very carefully the *first* task and see how workers react. Using the dashboard (or whatever interactive mechanism is available) we can see after a few minutes if workers have accepted work and submitted a few answers. This *attention* effect is extremely important as it can be used to sense if we will interest enough workers in our task. If the task fails to attract workers initially, then is unlikely that it will finish. The problem may be that the incentive is insufficient, that the instructions are not clear, the task is difficult, the content is uninteresting, or requires a lot of work. If workers are slow to accept the task, we should stop immediately and return to the design phase.

Depending on the end goal, the designer/developer must make work quality and completion time trade-offs. There is a delicate balance between compensation and filtering, with regard to the requester's time. Low compensation and/or a strict filtering procedure will drastically reduce the number of interested workers and hence will significantly increase a HIT's completion time.

One solution is to split long tasks and submit the smaller tasks in parallel. This approach has several advantages. First, the waiting time will decrease even though the total time spent on the tasks may not. Second, the overall time spent may also decrease because shorter tasks usually attract more workers. So, in summary, as common sense suggests, it is better to have many small tasks in the system than one very large task.

To schedule experiments effectively, it is better to submit shorter tasks first. This way, important implicit or explicit feedback from workers can be used to re-design larger experiments or tasks. This strategy is also helpful for debugging the task in the long run. Also, if something goes wrong, deleting tasks from a crowdsourcing platform is usually expensive in terms of both time and money. From a time perspective, the system needs to eliminate transactions based on the work that has been allocated. Furthermore, there are financial implications because the requester must pay for the portion of the work that has been completed.

When managing large data sets, it is useful to check if the same object needs to be re-labeled. For some applications, gathering fresh labels on duplicates may be useful. In others, re-assessing the same query—url pair is a waste of time and money. In terms of overall performance, some tasks may take longer than expected or, in the worst case, may not attract workers. This might be an indication that a particular task is not crowdsourcable in its current form.

Feedback about general communication between worker and requester is usually about a positive or negative experience working on a HIT. Workers tend to work for highly reputable requesters so those negative concerns must be resolved promptly. Good customer service will help build a reputation over time.

Adding a feedback loop by using an open-ended question is very valuable. It is possible to detect potential errors in the data set, operational issues, and learn how workers justify differently type of answers. We also found it useful to use the feedback as a way of fine tuning the HIT to keep improving the user experience.

Finally, as requesters, we need to monitor discussion forums (platform specific) and look out for problems regarding work posted. If there are issues with the HIT we need to address all types of feedback (e.g., poor guidelines, payments, passing grade, etc.) as soon as possible. It is all about good customer service.

6.7   SUMMARY OF PRACTICES

Not surprisingly, most the recommendations presented in the previous sections have been adopted from the software engineering community. To summarize, here is an incomplete list of suggestions when implementing large-scale labeling tasks.

- Do not ignore established software engineering principles and techniques. There is a large body of existing work in recommendations and best practices that can be useful when implementing hybrid human-machine systems.

- Eliminate errors early on. The methodology described in Section 6.2.3 is intended to help with detecting premature defects.

- Be skeptical about one size fits all solutions, especially quality control algorithms. While the algorithm may be theoretically correct, there are numerous items that can affect the choice of quality control techniques. Use the algorithm that fits the task best with respect to implementation cost and input data.

- Use an incremental approach for choosing the appropriate quality control solution.

- Working HITs are better. As observed by Brooks, "enthusiasm jumps when there is a running system" [36]. Having a simple HIT, albeit limited, so workers can perform work is better than waiting for the best solution.

- Faster but slower. There is a need to produce labels and the sooner the results are provided, the better. However, aggressive schedules and poor quality control techniques usually result in defective HITs, bad results, and a wasted budget.

- Data dependencies and overall technical debt. Machine Learning systems have the traditional maintenance problems of traditional software development plus additional ML-specific issues as observed by Sculley et al. [219].

- Manage expectations. It is possible that the HIT cannot be crowdsourced or the results are not as expected for a number of reasons. In those cases, it is good to have an exit strategy in place.

- Data collection and protection. Be open and honest about data collection and how such data will be used [254].

"All I know is that searching for my own name and then clicking on 'highly relevant' does wonders for my self-esteem."

6.8   SUMMARY

Data science solutions rely on sophisticated pipelines that include at some point, human input. There are tremendous opportunities for designing and implementing new crowd-based applications. However, there are some reservations when trying to implement new systems. Currently, available crowdsourcing platforms are somewhat rudimentary and impose many restrictions to developers as to the kind of HITs that can be implemented. This also has limitations for attracting and retaining workers.

Building crowd-based processing pipelines remains difficult and these difficulties need to be addressed by practitioners and researchers to advance the state of the art. In this chapter, we made a first step in identifying the many challenges that developers face today.

We proposed a simple methodology that contains three main phases: (1) coding using well known programming practices with placeholders for quality and payment (2) initial quality control with redundancy and payment structure; and (3) quality control improvements by adding human layer (expertise, retention, recruiting).

Pointers

There are some existing reports on methodologies and guidelines for specific scenarios mostly with respect to Mechanical Turk. General techniques for conducting experiments in Mechanical Turk are presented by Mason and Suri in the context of behavioral research [177]. Wang et al. provide a faceted analysis of crowdsourcing for collecting annotation for NLP [245]. Sabou et al. describe guidelines for crowdsourced corpus acquisition, also for NLP, and introduce the GATE Crowd plug-in [215, 216]. McCreadie et al. [180] present best practices for crowdsourcing relevance assessments in a real TREC setting using CrowdFlower. Vondrick et al. [242] enumerate best practices for video annotation and expand on limitations and expectations. Recommended practices for collecting data for human language technologies is summarized by Callison-Burch and Dredze [42]. Papoutsaki et al. [197] present an analysis of crowdsourcing strategies for novice requesters and provide guidelines for beginners. Andrew Ng's recent book provides great insight into structuring ML and AI projects and how to make things work [186].

The books by Brooks [37], Kernighan and Pike [131], McConnell [179], and Ousterhout [194] provide a lot of programming wisdom and practical advise. Other great references are the articles on software engineering by Boehm [28] and Brooks [36].

CHAPTER 7

Systems and Data Pipelines

> Sometimes the old ways are best, and
> they're certainly worth knowing well.
>
> Brian Kernighan

In this chapter we describe some examples of systems and data pipelines in different domains that contain human computation as an important component. Unfortunately, we cannot present a comprehensive list of existing systems. Instead, we describe examples that use crowdsourcing in a novel way starting with applications that utilize a commercial platform and later introduce systems that are designed around crowd-based computation.

"No, mechanical Turk."

7.1 EVALUATION

In many applications, evaluating the performance of a system requires human input and crowdsourcing is a feasible alternative to traditional methods that use a small set of experts for assessing performance. There is quite a bit of published research on different techniques and strategies for evaluating systems using crowdsourcing in many domains.

Information retrieval is one of those areas where crowdsourcing is used in practice for gathering relevance labels and performing search quality evaluation. Most of the crowdsourcing strategies use variations of HITs based on guidelines adapted from TREC [3, 7, 8, 44, 86, 102, 156, 223, 261, 262]. Other topics covered are human factors and label accuracy [128], demographics [127], user studies for web search [145], assessor errors in crowdsourcing [44], use of document content for aggregations [57], magnitudes [169], and quality control, in general [129].

When applying machine learning solutions in practice, it is not clear if a model has sensitive areas given the fact that it performs well according to certain evaluation metrics. How can we find defects in a predictive model? Human computation to the rescue. Parikh and Zitnick propose a *human-debugging* paradigm, where the goal is to use humans to identify problems in computational models and performance bottlenecks [200]. Under the assumption of a workflow that produces data at each step, each machine's output is replaced with output generated by humans. The overall performance of the system is then compared using combinations of machine and human components to measure accuracy.

An application of this paradigm is the work by Mottaghi et al. [184] that describes the use of human debugging for analyzing a conditional random field model for scene understanding as part of a computer vision task. By using humans at various stages of the proposed model, the authors were able to identify components of such a model that still have room for improvement.

Very related to the above examples is the identification of *unknown unknowns*, that is examples for which the model is wrong but is wrongly confident that it is correct. Thus, a classifier estimates the misclassification cost to be low but, in reality, the misclassification cost is high (Figure 7.1). The Beat the Machine (BTM) pattern, a game-like task where humans try to

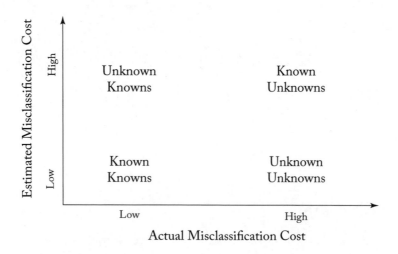

Figure 7.1: Four different classification scenarios based on estimated and actual misclassification costs: the *known knowns* (the model is mostly correct and returns a low expected misclassification cost); the *known unknowns* (the model is often wrong and returns a high expected misclassification cost); the unknown knowns (the model is often correct but returns high misclassification cost); and the *unknown unknowns* (the model is wrong but is wrongly confident that it is correct). Adapted from Attenberg et al. [14].

identify cases where the predictive model is wrong, is introduced by Attenberg et al. [14]. Instead of waiting for unknown errors to emerge, BTM uses crowdsourcing in a more proactive way to identify such cases. This is similar to hiring security experts to hack internal systems to ensure the security of an organization. The authors developed and tested five different designs when implementing the BTM task.

7.2 MACHINE TRANSLATION

Machine translation is one of the oldest subfields of artificial intelligence and consists of automatically converting text or speech from one language to another. Machine translation is a data-hungry task that depends on two languages and thus a good topic for testing crowdsourcing techniques. Historically the evaluation of translation quality has been extremely time-consuming and expensive to conduct.

Callison-Burch published one of the first papers that uses Mechanical Turk for recreating judgments from the WMT08 German-English translation task using preference voting and weighted voting schemes [40]. He showed that it was possible to use crowdsourcing for evaluating the quality of translation output.

A series of mechanisms for improving quality that includes redundant translation work, edition, and selection of best candidates is described by Zaidan and Callison-Burch [258]. The work is centered around techniques that increase the translation quality to near expert levels. The quality model includes three groups of features (sentence-level, worker-level, and ranking) and it was tested in an Urdu-English evaluation at a fraction of the cost of professionals.

Experiments with machine translation of Arabic Dialects and the construction of corpora for Levantine-English and Egyptian-English is described by Zbin et al. [259]. The size of the data set is about 1.5M words at a cost of about $0.03/word, which shows how scalable the process is.

7.3 HANDWRITTING RECOGNITION AND TRANSCRIPTION

Handwriting recognition is the task of transforming a language represented by graphical marks into its symbolic representation. Technology like optical character recognition that converts images into machine readable text is far from perfect and still a difficult task for humans and machines.

Little et al. [165] implement an iterative solution for handwriting recognition where workers build on or evaluate each other's work. The iterative implementation is possible by using the proposed TurKit toolkit.

The FamilySearch Indexing project is one of the largest crowdsourcing initiatives in the world[1] where volunteers transcribe billions of historical documents (mostly handwritten) in

[1]https://www.familysearch.org/

machine-readable format for genealogists and historians to study. Hansen et al. [93] study quality control mechanisms in FamilySearch Indexing and report that peer review took less time, but quality was, in some cases, inferior to arbitration. The authors also highlight the importance of expertise in the process.

Transcription of spoken language using a data set that contains utterances recorded by speaker category (male/female, native/non-native) is described by Marge et al. [173].

7.4   TAXONOMY CREATION

Taxonomy generation is a problem that usually requires a small set of domain experts working together revising and updating vocabulary, naming conventions, and devising the overall hierarchical structure. We briefly describe two systems, Cascade and Deluge, that are capable of creating a taxonomy from non-expert workers.

Cascade introduces three HIT primitives and a global structure inference algorithm to create taxonomies that are competitive in terms of quality and price [52]. The HIT primitives, modules, are `Generate` (asks worker to generate a category for an item), `SelectBest` (asks worker to identify the best category for an item), and `Categorize` (asks worker to vote whether the item belongs to a set of categories). Finally, an inference algorithm creates a global view of the individual categories. The authors implemented experiments with Mechanical Turk and reported a competitive output with respect to quality and price compared to the average expert cost.

Deluge is a refinement over Cascade that optimizes the assignment of category items to labels [31]. Deluge uses a probabilistic model that estimates the true value for an item and also controls which questions provide the maximum value. The authors implemented experiments with Mechanical Turk and reported comparable quality using 10% of the labor required by Cascade.

7.5   DATA ANALYSIS

There is very interesting work on using the crowd to analyze data sets. One such example is the work of André et al. [10] that implemented a two-stage process (re-representation and iterative clustering) for synthesizing an existing complex data set based on Wikipedia content. The work restricted workers to a single task and focused on novice workers.

Generating explanations for data and charts is important in data analysis and crowdsourcing can help in providing such explanations. Willett et al. [253] develop a workflow that selects charts and use workers to produce diverse explanations that can support the analysis. However, some explanations can be of low quality and the authors provide a number of strategies to improve results.

Chilton et al. [51] present Frenzy, a tool for data organization applied to conference session making. Frenzy breaks the task of session making into two problems: metadata elicitation and global constraint satisfaction. The system was tested with the CSCW 2014 program committee and the output was used to create the final conference schedule.

7.6 NEWS NEAR-DUPLICATE DETECTION

It is also possible to combine two different platforms as a mechanism to use separate workforces as in the evaluation of news duplication detection [4]. The authors use a two-phase approach using UHRS and Mechanical Turk in combination. First, a HIT for detecting if a document is a news article or not is executed in Mechanical Turk. Then, a different HIT for duplicate or non-duplicate assessment for news pairs runs in UHRS (Figure 7.2). The advantages are parallelization and different cost structure.

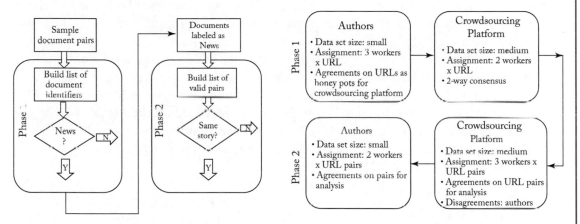

Figure 7.2: Two-phase approach for news near duplicate detection: (1) flowchart of crowdsourcing using two platforms and (2) flowchart of work quality.

The quality control strategy works as follows. Initially, a small data set is used to test the design of phase 1 experiments. Each URL was assessed by the authors and all disagreements resolved in person. The output was used as a honey-pot data set to check the quality of the same experiment template using a different crowd (UHRS). In this step, an overlapping medium-sized data set is used and each URL is assessed by two workers. All those URLs where both workers agree are then used to generate the URL pairs, which are the input for phase 2. In this second phase, each URL pair was assessed by three workers and for those few cases where at least two of the additional workers disagree with the initial judgment, the authors provided an extra label to compute the final list. The data set and HIT templates are available for download.[2]

---

[2]https://msropendata.com/datasets/45cfa711-1645-4747-8825-d8c62c7866df

7.7 ENTITY RESOLUTION

Entity resolution is the task of finding different records that refer to the same real-world entity from multiple sources. For example, there could be different ways of addressing the same person in documents such as "Bill Clinton" and "William Jefferson Clinton." Entity resolution is central to data quality, data cleaning, and database integration solutions.

CrowdER is a hybrid human-machine system in which machines are used to do an initial pass over the data, and then use the crowd to verify the most likely matching pair [246]. The main idea is to combine the efficiency of machine-based techniques with the answer quality that can be obtained from humans. Figure 7.3 describes the human-machine data workflow. The CrowdER system was tested using Mechanical Turk by running 8,000 HITs with a budget of $600. The authors report that the proposed hybrid approach achieves both good efficiency and a high-accuracy on a product and restaurant data sets. Another hybrid system for entity linking is ZenCrowd [60].

Corleone is a system for entity matching that uses the notion of hands-off crowdsourcing. That is, the idea is to crowdsource the entire workflow for a task and requires no software developers as part of the workflow process [85]. Compared to other crowd-based entity matching systems that require engineering time to code heuristic rules to reduce the number of matches, Corleone uses the crowd to train a machine learner matcher. Corleone was tested on Mechanical Turk with three different data sets, including an electronics products data set with varying matches between Amazon and Walmart.

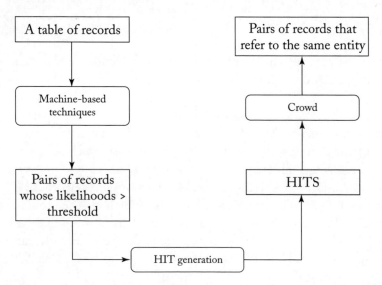

Figure 7.3: Hybrid human-machine workflow in CrowdER. Figure adapted from Wang et al. [246].

7.8 CLASSIFICATION

Moving into more real-world examples, there are few reports about large-scale data sets and crowdsourcing. Chimera is a system for classifying tens of millions of products into 5,000 product types at Walmart. This is a good example of a hybrid human-machine system that combines machine learning, rules, crowdsourcing, analysts, and developers to solve a classification problem in a cost-effective way [229]. The system uses multiple classifiers (kNN, Naive-Bayes, Perceptron) and rule-based classifiers developed by in-house analysts. Crowdsourcing is used for evaluating the performance of the classification output and forward the problematic cases to the analysts. The analysts then update the rules, correct the labels, and incorporate the feedback into the system for the next round of classification with the end goal to keep improving quality continuously.

7.9 IMAGE AND SPEECH

Image labeling has been one of the most used domains for human computation and the famous ESP game is such example. Nowak and Ruger [189] performed many experiments on inter-rater agreement in assessing ground truth of existing multi-labeled images and report that the work quality of workers on Mechanical Turk is comparable to experts.

Branson et al. [32] propose a hybrid human-computer classification system that poses questions based on visual properties that are easy to answer by humans. The human-in-the-loop solution was tested with the Birds-200 data set on Mechanical Turk and results show that human input improves performance.

Digital assistant that uses speech recognition to provide answers to users through phones and voice recognition applications is one of the latest trends in end-consumer products. State-of-the-art speech recognition systems use lots of data for training and evaluation. The work by Novotney and Callison-Burch use Mechanical Turk to reduce the cost of transcribing conversational telephone speech data [188]. They observe that when a domain is new there is no ground truth to use as reference, so they develop techniques for estimating worker skill that is then used for selecting good workers.

7.10 INFORMATION EXTRACTION

Information Extraction is the task of automatically extracting structured information such as entities, relationships, and attributes from unstructured or semi-structured textual sources.

Kumar et al [138] introduce Higgins, a system that integrates an information extraction engine with a crowd-based human computation engine for knowledge acquisition. Higgins uses the information extraction phase to derive candidates for entity-relationship facts. The noisy and incomplete candidates from the previous stage are used by the human computation engine to generate a HIT in the form of a game. The game structure consists of asking workers to fill in missing slots and allocates points for answers. The main techniques were implemented and tested in CrowdFlower.

Wernicke, proposed by Han et al. [92], is a system that supports web page annotation for information extraction and use behavioral features to predict work quality. The system consists of a browser extension module and a quality control module. The browser extension has a behavior logger feature that records workers' crowdsourcing behaviors, including mouse-clicking, mouse over, scrolling, etc. A weighted majority voting method is used for aggregating annotations from multiple workers. By running experiments, the authors showed that a quality-control model using workers' behavioral signals is more effective than using workers' historical performance.

7.11   RABJ

Redundant Array of Brains in a Jar (RABJ) is a question answering service designed to simplify the collection of human input for Freebase, a collaborative knowledge base [137]. RABJ is an example of tiered workforce, that is, paid contractors or hired editors and volunteers. The system is content agnostic and the smallest unit of work is a question that requires human input data. Workers are not anonymous allowing the requester to have transparent communications channels and evaluations. The system has been used in production and the authors reported that 2.3 million judgments were collected on 1.7 million unique answers. Freebase has been acquired by Google.

The Freebase project has a number of interesting takeaways with respect to managing crowds and we share a few:

- Long-term relationships with judges are beneficial.

- Time-based compensation is effective.

- Fewer options lead to less conflict.

- Incentives for volunteers are different than paid judges.

7.12   WORKFLOWS

As we have seen in this book, complex workflows or data pipelines are common in crowdsourcing settings. An interesting research topic is how to automatically control the components of such workflows.

The already-mentioned systems, Chimera and Corleone, are home-grown workflows solutions implemented for a specific domain like e-commerce. Both systems work at scale and have been deployed in real-world scenarios. Sun et al. [229] also outline lessons learned and we highlight a couple of interesting observations: things break down at scale and the importance of monitoring progress.

The work by Dai et al. [54] proposes to construct artificial intelligence agents for workflow optimization and control. The authors describe three agents (TurKontrol$_0$, TurKontrol$_1$, and AgentHunt) for different scenarios and present implementation details for Mechanical Turk.

Kulkarni et al. [142] describe Turkomatic, a meta-workflow that recruits workers to help requesters in planning and solving complex tasks. The system implements the *price-divide-solve* pattern that asks workers to divide complex steps into simpler ones until they are simple enough so they can be solved.

CrowdForge [136], a general purpose framework inspired by MapReduce, is used in a collaborative writing task and researching a purchase decision. The prototype uses Mechanical Turk as a backend and it doesn't support iteration or recursion. However, the idea that complex work can be partitioned into smaller independent pieces that can be processed by the crowd is a neat idea.

7.13 SUMMARY

We presented some examples of difficult problems that can be solved by including human computation as a component of a system. Some of those applications use existing platforms like Mechanical Turk, CrowdFlower, or a combination thereof. In other cases, we can see the importance of modularization and the power of designing HITs that can be composed as part of a solution. Kittur et al. [135] propose a framework for crowd work and describe the main research challenges.

CHAPTER 8

Looking Ahead

> Programming will remain very difficult,
> because once we have freed ourselves from
> the circumstantial cumbersomeness, we will
> find ourselves free to tackle the problems
> that are now well beyond our programming
> capacity.
>
> Edsger Dijkstra

We conclude with a discussion of emerging topics in crowdsourcing research, current issues, and challenges that researchers and practitioners are addressing. We are in the early days of hybrid computation systems and using a "command-line" paradigm for implementing HITs. We need to move to better infrastructure and platforms that can improve productivity and allow programmers to implement novel applications.

8.1   CROWDS AND SOCIAL NETWORKS

We like to think of a social network as a good source of workers who have a specific expertise and are not anonymous. While most of the research work has focused on simple tasks or questions, there is quite a bit of potential in this area. There are two important concepts that are common in this line of research: social routing [73], a task is delegated to a specific community or to the crowd, and expert finding. Expertise detection is difficult as tasks may require different set of skills and, in some cases, experts are available in different sources, which requires integration and normalization across abilities. It would be interesting to see also the inclusion of social search [76] as another aspect to this problem.

There has been work on using social networks for question-answering tasks, like the case of Aardvark that routes a question to the right person [100]. The questions that were asked in Aardvark are mostly subjective as users usually find them difficult to get answer using a web search engine.

Jeong et al. [116] describe MSR Answers, a system that uses the crowd to identify question tweets with the initial goal of automating question-answering. While using Twitter as source may have limitations, the evaluation shows positive feedback for a crowd-powered embedded search engine.

The work by Bozzon et al. [29] tackles the problem of selecting top-k experts from different social networks (Facebook, Twitter, LinkedIn). Besides user profile information, user activity and other behavioral data are useful signals for assessing expertise.

CrowdStar is a general model for task routing and expertise detection in online crowd-sourced communities [190]. The goal of the system is to find the best-matching crowd for a given task. The system indexes the dynamically changing crowd expertise and uses this knowledge index to route tasks to the right crowds and individual users. To avoid overloading a specific worker a social load-balancing strategy is used. The intent of this approach, called social task routing, is to find competent people that answer a problem for which an otherwise definite answer does not exist (e.g., via Web search).

Pick-A-Crowd is a system that pushes tasks to the right workers instead of letting workers select which tasks they want to work on [65]. User profiles are constructed based on workers' online social network activities. The system was tested using OpenTurk, a native Facebook application that pushes tasks to selected workers and collects the answers.

Collaboration is another topic that has potential for new applications based on crowds. Examples are Turkomatic, a crowdsourcing tool where workers and the requester collaboratively design and execute a workflow [142] and Frenzy, a collaborative web interface for managing tasks around the organization of a conference [51]. Another system called Revolt, proposed by Chang et al. [46], enables groups of workers to collaboratively label data through three states (vote, explain, categorize) without any specific guidelines. A different approach is introduced by Kim et al. [132] where they observe that developing good workflows is a hard problem and introduce a technique that loops between two phases: reflection of crowd progress and revising the work. They implement the technique in Mechanical Novel, a system that crowdsources short stories in Mechanical Turk.

We briefly mentioned GWAPs in Chapter 1, but we have not covered the topic in this book. There is tremendous potential in designing and implement GWAPs for labeling and related problems [150, 206], and we look forward to seeing further adoption of games in practice.

8.2   INTERACTIVE AND REAL-TIME CROWDSOURCING

Nowadays we are used to rapid response times from any device and a valid open question is: can crowd-powered system support interactivity or real-time processing?

The Soylent system is a word processing interface that enables writers to call a crowd, Mechanical Turk in this case, to help shorten, proofread, and edit documents in Microsoft Word [25]. The system introduced the Find-Fix-Verify crowd programming pattern described in Section 4.5. The main idea behind Soylent is the use of embedding paid crowd workers in an interactive user interface to support document editing tasks on demand. A common item on this line of work is latency. In the case of Soylent the authors report that lag times are "on the order of minutes to hours" due to worker demographics and availability.

Real-time captioning provides people with hearing problems access to speech text as the event takes place. Some problems with using crowdsourcing for real-time captioning is that workers cannot keep up with natural speaking rates. A solution to this problem is TimeWarp, a technique that allows each worker to type slowed clips played as close to real-time as possible [147].

Other innovative examples are Chorus, a crowd-powered conversational assistant [148], real-time image search using mobile devices [255], and applications that use on-demand synchronous crowds, where workers arrive and work simultaneously [24]. André et al. [11] study coordination models and find that sequential work structures seem to work best.

8.3 PROGRAMMING LANGUAGES

In his "No Silver Bullet" article, Brooks identified the use of high-level programming languages as one of the most powerful past breakthroughs for software productivity, reliability, and simplicity [36]. We are still in the very early stages of crowdsourcing and human computation where there is a clear need for a high-level programming language that can help programmers be more productive and enable the creation of new software.

There has been some research on programming languages and toolkits but, in general, software development environments and programming models are open areas that we hope to see important advancements in the near future. An example of how to implement hybrid computation is TurKit, a toolkit for programming algorithmic human computation while maintaining an imperative programming style is introduced by Little et al. [166]. TurKit uses a crash-and-rerun programming model suited to long running processes where local computation is cheap, and remote work is costly (HITs). Similar approaches are examined in Little et al. [164] and Miller et al. [183].

A domain-specific language (DSL) or "little language" is a computer language specialized to a particular application domain and they can be very useful. AutoMan is a great example of how programming with human computation should look like [20]. AutoMan is a DSL embedded in Scala that includes an automatic scheduler that maximizes parallelism while staying under budget. The DSL uses an adaptive approach for quality control using the programmer's confidence threshold and consensus.

Another DSL called VoxPL targets scenarios where there is a need to implement estimation tasks. That is, tasks that require workers to approximate a continuous value [19]. VoxPL is also embedded within Scala and consists of a grammar for programmers to create and combine estimates.

Most of the current work around programming extensions is still modeled after Mechanical Turk and not ready yet for real-world applications. Programming languages, interactive development environments that support hybrid computation, and code generators are unexplored areas that can have a huge impact on this new field.

8.4   DATABASES AND CROWD-POWERED ALGORITHMS

It should be obvious by now, but a great advantage of crowdsourcing is the ability to collect data for all sorts of domains at scale very fast. Once such data sets are collected databases come to the rescue as proven technology for storing, and querying. The database community has been paying close attention to crowd-based application and developed some interesting prototypes and concepts that use crowdsourcing as features or added functionality.

CrowdDB, the first system that uses human computation for processing queries that traditional databases or search engines cannot answer, is presented by Franklin et al. [80]. CrowdDB offers basic quality control features, but we expect adoption of more advanced techniques as those systems become more available within the community.

Qurk is a system for writing SQL-like queries to manage crowdsourcing workflows [172]. A declarative query model that operates on humans and databases, called hQuery, is described in [199]. Algorithms for filtering data properties that can be verified by humans are presented in Parameswaran et al. [198].

8.5   FAIRNESS, BIAS, AND REPRODUCIBILITY

As machine learning solutions are deployed in production systems, there is a growing concern in both academia and the field about the risks and implications for such hunger data systems. A new set of conferences like ACM FAT (`fatconference.org`) and workshops have emerged to track the state of the art. We briefly outline some research avenues.

Barbosa and Chen [17] propose a framework that allocates tasks to workers by considering human factors such as demographics and minimum wage by country. The framework was implemented in Figure Eight using around 2,000 workers and collected 160,000 labels.

In this book we've covered many techniques and described different applications. Unfortunately, in the real-world there are no standards to document how the labels were created, how to reproduce the process, and if there are any ethical considerations. Gebru et al. [84] propose the idea of datasheets for datasets, similar to standards used in the electronics industry.

Sutton et al. [232] propose the problem of providing a summary of the differences between two data sets in the context of data analysis tasks. We believe that similar *data diffs* tasks can be applied to labeling data sets.

8.6   AN INCOMPLETE LIST OF REQUIREMENTS FOR INFRASTRUCTURE

The rudimentary state of current platforms enforces limitations on the kind of tasks that can be accomplish and the recruitment of good workers. How would the next generation of platforms look like? As requesters, if we have to use new infrastructure for implementing HITs, which features we would like to have in place? As workers, what would be the expectations for contributing our time and effort? As infrastructure owners what do we need to build? In this subsection we outline some initial requirements.

As requesters we have two main goals to fulfill: implement the right task that produces the labels that we are looking for and, at the same time, make it appealing to workers. The task needs to grab attention. Without interesting content and proper incentive, people won't complete the task and we won't get our labels.

- Tools that help implement easy to use interfaces that allow any human with minimum instructions to perform a well-defined task. The standard form-based interface to collect data is limited and not always suitable for tasks that require interactivity.

- Capacity to pay for work in different currencies and to setup up other incentives like points.

- Ability to manage workers in different levels of expertise including spammers and bots.

- Ability to mix different pools of workers based on different profile and expertise levels.

- Honey-pot management and incremental qualification tests based on expertise and past performance.

Workers need a good search feature and personalized recommendations to find the most relevant task. Task with low usability and subpar incentives should not be the norm and workers should be able to provide feedback. The elastic human workforce is the planet so cultural and multilingual characteristic need be part of the task design.

- According to behavioral economics, it is important for people to see the value in the work they perform. Money is the most obvious incentive, however, it should be possible to use other equivalents like points, or reputation as currency that workers can use to see that their work is meaningful.

- Personalized routing/recommendation of similar tasks based on past behavior, content, and/or requester.

- Requester rating based on payment performance, rejected work, and overall task difficulty. A worker should be able to rate the quality of work and the quality of the requester.

- Ability to comment on a task.

- Work categorization. Similarly to a job search site, all work that is available should be classified.

As platform owner, in addition to the items listed above, a few more specific requirements that benefit workers and requesters.

- Spam detection built in the system.

- Payments including international markets.

- Ability to plug-in user-defined quality control.

- High-level language for designing tasks that supports interactivity.

8.7   SUMMARY

Crowdsourcing and systems that are powered by hybrid computation are here to stay. Researchers and practitioners on different areas of information technology are finding crowd-computing as an alternative way to collect data to solve problems efficiently. The more we crowdsource tasks and implement different HITs, the more we learn about potential features and useful scenarios.

Writing programs that can use human computation successfully requires a solid framework that uses established programming principles. A mix of different skills and expertise are required for implementing human computation-based solutions, e.g., social and behavioral science, human factors, algorithms, economics, distributed systems, and statistics. It is important to know our own limitations and be ready to collaborate with other teams.

"Ernie is his own crowd."

Bibliography

[1] Ittai Abraham, Omar Alonso, Vasilis Kandylas, Rajesh Patel, Steven Shelford, and Aleksandrs Slivkins. How many workers to ask?: Adaptive exploration for collecting high quality labels. In *Proc. of SIGIR*, pages 473–482, 2016. DOI: 10.1145/2911451.2911514 28, 56, 59, 60

[2] Mohammad Allahbakhsh, Boualem Benatallah, Aleksandar Ignjatovic, Hamid R. Motahari Nezhad, Elisa Bertino, and Schahram Dustdar. Quality control in crowdsourcing systems: Issues and directions. *IEEE Internet Computing*, 17(2):76–81, 2013. DOI: 10.1109/mic.2013.20 37

[3] Omar Alonso and Ricardo A. Baeza-Yates. Design and implementation of relevance assessments using crowdsourcing. In *Proc. of ECIR*, pages 153–164, 2011. DOI: 10.1007/978-3-642-20161-5_16 89

[4] Omar Alonso, Dennis Fetterly, and Mark S. Manasse. Duplicate news story detection revisited. In *Proc. of AIRS*, pages 203–214, 2013. DOI: 10.1007/978-3-642-45068-6_18 93

[5] Omar Alonso, Catherine C. Marshall, and Marc Najork. Are some tweets more interesting than others? #HardQuestion. In *Proc. of HCIR*, pages 2:1–2:10, 2013. DOI: 10.1145/2528394.2528396 46

[6] Omar Alonso, Catherine C. Marshall, and Marc Najork. Debugging a crowdsourced task with low inter-rater agreement. In *Proc. of JCDL*, pages 101–110, 2015. DOI: 10.1145/2756406.2757741 47, 79

[7] Omar Alonso and Stefano Mizzaro. Can we get rid of TREC assessors? Using mechanical turk for relevance assessment. In *Proc. of Future of IR Evaluation Workshop*, pages 557–566, 2009. 89

[8] Omar Alonso and Stefano Mizzaro. Using crowdsouring for TREC relevance assessment. *Information Processing and Management*, 48(6):1053–1066, 2012. DOI: 10.1016/j.ipm.2012.01.004 89

[9] Omar Alonso, Daniel E. Rose, and Benjamin Stewart. Crowdsourcing for relevance evaluation. *SIGIR Forum*, 42(2):9–15, 2008. DOI: 10.1145/1480506.1480508 3

[10] Paul André, Aniket Kittur, and Steven P. Dow. Crowd synthesis: Extracting categories and clusters from complex data. In *Proc. of CSCW*, pages 989–998, 2014. DOI: 10.1145/2531602.2531653 92

[11] Paul André, Robert E. Kraut, and Aniket Kittur. Effects of simultaneous and sequential work structures on distributed collaborative interdependent tasks. In *Proc. of CHI*, pages 139–148, 2014. DOI: 10.1145/2556288.2557158 101

[12] Judd Antin and Aaron D. Shaw. Social desirability bias and self-reports of motivation: A study of Amazon mechanical turk in the U.S. and India. In *Proc. of CHI*, pages 2925–2934, 2012. DOI: 10.1145/2207676.2208699 69

[13] Ron Artstein and Massimo Poesio. Inter-coder agreement for computational linguistics. *Computational Linguistics*, pages 555–596, 2008. DOI: 10.1162/coli.07-034-r2 43

[14] Joshua Attenberg, Panos Ipeirotis, and Foster J. Provost. Beat the machine: Challenging humans to find a predictive model's "unknown unknowns". *Journal of Data and Information Quality*, 6(1):1:1–1:17, 2015. DOI: 10.1145/2700832 90, 91

[15] Yoram Bachrach, Thore Graepel, Tom Minka, and John Guiver. How to grade a test without knowing the answers—a Bayesian graphical model for adaptive crowdsourcing and aptitude testing. In *Proc. of ICML*, 2012. 63

[16] Piyush Bansal, Carsten Eickhoff, and Thomas Hofmann. Active content-based crowdsourcing task selection. In *Proc. of CIKM*, pages 529–538, 2016. DOI: 10.1145/2983323.2983716 63

[17] Nata Barbosa and Monchu Chen. Rehumanized crowdsourcing: A labeling framework addressing bias and ethics in machine learning. In *Proc. of CHI*, 2019. DOI: 10.1145/3290605.3300773 102

[18] Kimberly A. Barchard and John Williams. Practical advice for conducting ethical online experiments and questionnaires for United States psychologists. *Behavior Research Methods*, 40(4):1111–1128, November 2008. DOI: 10.3758/brm.40.4.1111 71

[19] Daniel W. Barowy, Emery D. Berger, Daniel G. Goldstein, and Siddharth Suri. VoxPL: Programming with the wisdom of the crowd. In *Proc. of CHI*, pages 2347–2358, 2017. DOI: 10.1145/3025453.3026025 101

[20] Daniel W. Barowy, Charlie Curtsinger, Emery D. Berger, and Andrew McGregor. AutoMan: A platform for integrating human-based and digital computation. *Communications of the ACM*, 59(6):102–109, 2016. DOI: 10.1145/2384616.2384663 101

[21] Jeff Barr and Luis-Felipe Cabrera. AI gets a brain. *ACM Queue*, 4(4):24–29, 2006. DOI: 10.1145/1142055.1142067 3

[22] Tara S. Behrend, David J. Sharek, Adam W. Meade, and Eric N. Wiebe. The viability of crowdsourcing for survey research. *Behavior Research Methods*, 43(3):800–813, 2011. DOI: 10.1037/e518362013-534 66

[23] Janine Berg. Income security in the on-demand economy: Findings and policy lessons from a survey of crowdworkers. *Comparative Labor Law and Policy Journal*, 37(3), 2016. 67

[24] Michael S. Bernstein, Joel Brandt, Robert C. Miller, and David R. Karger. Crowds in two seconds: Enabling realtime crowd-powered interfaces. In *Proc. of UIST*, pages 33–42, 2011. DOI: 10.1145/2047196.2047201 101

[25] Michael S. Bernstein, Greg Little, Robert C. Miller, Björn Hartmann, Mark S. Ackerman, David R. Karger, David Crowell, and Katrina Panovich. Soylent: A word processor with a crowd inside. *Communications of the ACM*, 58(8):85–94, 2015. DOI: 10.1145/2791285 57, 100

[26] Roi Blanco, Harry Halpin, Daniel M. Herzig, Peter Mika, Jeffrey Pound, Henry S. Thompson, and Duc Thanh Tran. Repeatable and reliable search system evaluation using crowdsourcing. In *Proceeding of SIGIR*, pages 923–932, 2011. DOI: 10.1145/2009916.2010039 63

[27] Michael Bloodgood and Chris Callison-Burch. Bucking the trend: Large-scale cost-focused active learning for statistical machine translation. In *Proc. of ACL*, pages 854–864, 2010. 57, 63

[28] Barry W. Boehm. A view of 20th and 21st century software engineering. In *Proc. of ICSE*, pages 12–29, 2006. DOI: 10.1145/1134285.1134288 87

[29] Alessandro Bozzon, Marco Brambilla, Stefano Ceri, Mattco Silvestri, and Giuliano Vesci. Choosing the right crowd: Expert finding in social networks. In *Proc. of EDBT*, pages 637–648, 2013. DOI: 10.1145/2452376.2452451 100

[30] Norman Bradburn, Seymour Sudman, and Brian Wansink. *Asking Questions*. Jossey-Bass, 2004. 36

[31] Jonathan Bragg, Mausam, and Daniel S. Weld. Crowdsourcing multi-label classification for taxonomy creation. In *Proc. of HCOMP*, 2013. 92

[32] Steve Branson, Catherine Wah, Florian Schroff, Boris Babenko, Peter Welinder, Pietro Perona, and Serge Belongie. Visual recognition with humans in the loop. In *Proc. of ECCV*, pages 438–451, 2010. DOI: 10.1007/978-3-642-15561-1_32 95

[33] Alice M. Brawley and Cynthia L. S. Pury. Work experiences on MTurk: Job satisfaction, turnover, and information sharing. *Computers in Human Behavior*, 54:531–546, 2016. DOI: 10.1016/j.chb.2015.08.031 68

[34] Anthony Brew, Derek Greene, and Padraig Cunningham. Using crowdsourcing and active learning to track sentiment in online media. In *Proc. of ECAI*, pages 145–150, 2010. 63

[35] Carla E. Brodley and Mark A. Friedl. Identifying mislabeled training data. *Journal of Artificial Intelligence Research*, 11:131–167, 1999. DOI: 10.1613/jair.606 63

[36] Frederick P. Brooks, Jr. No silver bullet—essence and accidents of software engineering. *IEEE Computer*, 20(4):10–19, 1987. DOI: 10.1109/mc.1987.1663532 86, 87, 101

[37] Frederick P. Brooks, Jr. *The Mythical Man-Month—Essays on Software Engineering*, 2nd ed., Addison-Wesley, 1995. DOI: 10.1109/mahc.1996.539925 87

[38] Michael Buhrmester, Tract Kwang, and Samuel Gosling. Amazon's mechanical turk: A new source of inexpensive, yet high-quality, data? *Perspectives on Psychological Science*, 6:3–5, 2011. DOI: 10.1037/e527772014-223 66

[39] Trevor Burnham and Rahul Sami. A reputation system for selling human computation. In *Proc. of HCOMP Workshop*, 2009. DOI: 10.1145/1600150.1600169 63

[40] Chris Callison-Burch. Fast, cheap, and creative: Evaluating translation quality using Amazon mechanical turk. In *Proc. of EMNLP*, pages 286–295, 2009. DOI: 10.3115/1699510.1699548 3, 63, 91

[41] Chris Callison-Burch. Crowd-workers: Aggregating information across turkers to help them find higher paying work. In *Proc. of HCOMP*, 2014. 67

[42] Chris Callison-Burch and Mark Dredze. Creating speech and language data with Amazon's mechanical turk. In *Proc. of MTurk@HLT-NAACL*, pages 1–12, 2010. 87

[43] Donald Campbell. Task complexity: A review and analysis. *Academy of Management Review*, 13(1):40–52, 1988. DOI: 10.2307/258353 27

[44] Ben Carterette and Ian Soboroff. The effect of assessor error on IR system evaluation. In *Proc. of SIGIR*, pages 539–546, 2010. DOI: 10.1145/1835449.1835540 89, 90

[45] Jesse Chandler, Pam Mueller, and Gabriele Paolacci. Nonnaïveté among Amazon mechanical turk workers: Consequences and solutions for behavioral researchers. *Behavior Research Methods*, 46(1):112–130, March 2014. DOI: 10.3758/s13428-013-0365-7 66

[46] Joseph Chee Chang, Saleema Amershi, and Ece Kamar. Revolt: Collaborative crowd-sourcing for labeling machine learning datasets. In *Proc. of the CHI Conference on Human Factors in Computing Systems*, pages 2334–2346, Denver, CO, May 06–11, 2017. 100 DOI: 10.1145/3025453.3026044

[47] Alessandro Checco, Kevin Roitero, Eddy Maddalena, Stefano Mizzaro, and Gianluca Demartini. Let's agree to disagree: Fixing agreement measures for crowdsourcing. In *Proc. of HCOMP*, pages 11–20, 2017. 51

[48] Xi Chen, Qihang Lin, and Dengyong Zhou. Optimistic knowledge gradient policy for optimal budget allocation in crowdsourcing. In *Proc. of ICML*, pages 64–72, 2013. 63

[49] Justin Cheng, Jaime Teevan, and Michael S. Bernstein. Measuring crowdsourc-ing effort with error-time curves. In *Proc. of CHI*, pages 1365–1374, 2015. DOI: 10.1145/2702123.2702145 28

[50] Lydia B. Chilton, John J. Horton, Robert C. Miller, and Shiri Azenkot. Task search in a human computation market. In *Proc. of HCOMP*, pages 1–9, 2010. DOI: 10.1145/1837885.1837889 68

[51] Lydia B. Chilton, Juho Kim, Paul André, Felicia Cordeiro, James A. Landay, Daniel S. Weld, Steven P. Dow, Robert C. Miller, and Haoqi Zhang. Frenzy: Collaborative data organization for creating conference sessions. In *Proc. of CHI*, pages 1255–1264, 2014. DOI: 10.1145/2556288.2557375 92, 100

[52] Lydia B. Chilton, Greg Little, Darren Edge, Daniel S. Weld, and James A. Landay. Cascade: crowdsourcing taxonomy creation. In *Proc. of CHI*, pages 1999–2008, 2013. DOI: 10.1145/2470654.2466265 92

[53] Anand Inasu Chittilappilly, Lei Chen, and Sihem Amer-Yahia. A survey of general-purpose crowdsourcing techniques. *IEEE Transactions on Knowledge Data Engineering*, 28(9):2246–2266, 2016. DOI: 10.1109/tkde.2016.2555805 62

[54] Peng Dai, Christopher H. Lin, Mausam, and Daniel S. Weld. POMDP-based con-trol of workflows for crowdsourcing. *Artificial Intelligence*, 202:52–85, 2013. DOI: 10.1016/j.artint.2013.06.002 97

[55] Peng Dai, Jeffrey M. Rzeszotarski, Praveen Paritosh, and Ed H. Chi. And now for some-thing completely different: Improving crowdsourcing workflows with micro-diversions. In *Proc. of CSCW*, pages 628–638, 2015. DOI: 10.1145/2675133.2675260 81

[56] Florian Daniel, Pavel Kucherbaev, Cinzia Cappiello, Boualem Benatallah, and Moham-mad Allahbakhsh. Quality control in crowdsourcing: A survey of quality attributes, as-sessment techniques and assurance actions. *ACM Computing Surveys*, 51(1):1–40, 2018. DOI: 10.1145/3148148 37

[57] Martin Davtyan, Carsten Eickhoff, and Thomas Hofmann. Exploiting document content for efficient aggregation of crowdsourcing votes. In *Proc. of CIKM*, pages 783–790, 2015. DOI: 10.1145/2806416.2806460 90

[58] A. P. Dawid and A. M. Skene. Maximum likelihood estimation of observer error-rates using the EM algorithm. *Journal of the Royal Statistical Society. Series C (Applied Statistics)*, pages 20–28, 1979. DOI: 10.2307/2346806 45, 59

[59] Ofer Dekel and Ohad Shamir. Vox populi: Collecting high-quality labels from a crowd. In *Proc. of COLT*, 2009. 59

[60] Gianluca Demartini, Djellel Eddine Difallah, and Philippe Cudré-Mauroux. ZenCrowd: Leveraging probabilistic reasoning and crowdsourcing techniques for large-scale entity linking. In *Proc. WWW*, pages 469–478, 2012. DOI: 10.1145/2187836.2187900 94

[61] Gianluca Demartini, Djellel Eddine Difallah, Ujwal Gadiraju, and Michele Catasta. An introduction to hybrid human-machine information systems. *Foundations and Trends in Web Science*, 7(1):1–87, 2017. DOI: 10.1561/1800000025 14

[62] William Edwards Deming. *Some Theory of Sampling*. Dover, 1950. 36, 78

[63] Jia Deng, Olga Russakovsky, Jonathan Krause, Michael S. Bernstein, Alexander C. Berg, and Fei-Fei Li. Scalable multi-label annotation. In *Proc. of CHI*, pages 3099–3102, 2014. DOI: 10.1145/2556288.2557011 63

[64] Djellel Eddine Difallah, Michele Catasta, Gianluca Demartini, Panagiotis G. Ipeirotis, and Philippe Cudré-Mauroux. The dynamics of micro-task crowdsourcing: The case of Amazon MTurk. In *Proc. of WWW*, pages 238–247, 2015. DOI: 10.1145/2740908.2744109 66

[65] Djellel Eddine Difallah, Gianluca Demartini, and Philippe Cudré-Mauroux. Pick-a-crowd: Tell me what you like, and I'll tell you what to do. In *Proc. of WWW*, pages 367–374, 2013. DOI: 10.1145/2488388.2488421 100

[66] Djellel Eddine Difallah, Elena Filatova, and Panos Ipeirotis. Demographics and dynamics of mechanical turk workers. In *Proc. of WSDM*, pages 135–143, 2018. DOI: 10.1145/3159652.3159661 66

[67] Anhai Doan, Raghu Ramakrishnan, and Alon Y. Halevy. Crowdsourcing systems on the world-wide web. *Communications of the ACM*, 54, April 2011. DOI: 10.1145/1924421.1924442 14

[68] Sveva Besana Donghui Feng and Remi Zajac. Acquiring high quality non-expert knowledge from on-demand workforce. In *Workshop on the People's Web Meets NLP*, 2009. DOI: 10.3115/1699765.1699773 63

[69] Pinar Donmez, Jaime G. Carbonell, and Jeff G. Schneider. A probabilistic framework to learn from multiple annotators with time-varying accuracy. In *Proc. of SIAM*, pages 826–837, 2010. DOI: 10.1137/1.9781611972801.72 63

[70] Steven Dow, Anand Pramod Kulkarni, Scott R. Klemmer, and Björn Hartmann. Shepherding the crowd yields better work. In *Proc. of CSCW*, pages 1013–1022, 2012. DOI: 10.1145/2145204.2145355 57

[71] Julie S. Downs, Mandy B. Holbrook, Steve Sheng, and Lorrie Faith Cranor. Are your participants gaming the system?: Screening mechanical turk workers. In *Proc. of CHI*, pages 2399–2402, 2010. DOI: 10.1145/1753326.1753688 42

[72] Ryan Drapeau, Lydia B. Chilton, Jonathan Bragg, and Daniel S. Weld. MicroTalk: Using argumentation to improve crowdsouricng accuracy. In *Proc. of HCOMP*, pages 32–41, 2016. 58

[73] Schahram Dustdar and Martin Gaedke. The social routing principle. *IEEE Internet Computing*, 15(4):80–83, 2011. DOI: 10.1109/mic.2011.97 99

[74] Carsten Eickhoff. Cognitive biases in crowdsourcing. In *Proc. of WSDM*, pages 162–170, 2018. DOI: 10.1145/3159652.3159654 25

[75] Avshalom Elmalech, David Sarne, Esther David, and Chen Hajaj. Extending workers' attention span through dummy events. In *Proc. of HCOMP*, 2016. 55

[76] Brynn M. Evans and Ed H. Chi. An elaborated model of social search. *Information Processing and Management*, 46(6):656–678, 2010. DOI: 10.1016/j.ipm.2009.10.012 99

[77] Boi Faltings, Radu Jurca, Pearl Pu, and Bao Duy Tran. Incentives to counter bias in human computation. In *Proc. of the HCOMP*, 2014. 62

[78] Alek Felstiner. Working the crowd: Employment and labor law in the crowdsourcing industry. *32 Berkeley J. Emp. and Lab. L.*, 2011. 71

[79] Floyd Fowler. *Improving Survey Questions*. Sage Publications, 1995. 20, 36

[80] Michael J. Franklin, Donald Kossmann, Tim Kraska, Sukriti Ramesh, and Reynold Xin. CrowdDB: Answering queries with crowdsourcing. In *Proc. of SIGMOD*, pages 61–72, 2011. DOI: 10.1145/1989323.1989331 102

[81] Ujwal Gadiraju. Make hay while the crowd shines: Towards efficient crowdsourcing on the Web. In *Proc. of WWW*, pages 493–497, 2015. DOI: 10.1145/2740908.2741748 63

[82] Ujwal Gadiraju, Ricardo Kawase, Stefan Dietze, and Gianluca Demartini. Understanding malicious behavior in crowdsourcing platforms: The case of online surveys. In *Proc. of CHI*, pages 1631–1640, 2015. DOI: 10.1145/2702123.2702443 63

[83] Ujwal Gadiraju, Jie Yang, and Alessandro Bozzon. Clarity is a worthwhile quality: On the role of task clarity in microtask crowdsourcing. In *Proc. of HT*, pages 5–14, 2017. DOI: 10.1145/3078714.3078715 26

[84] Timnit Gebru, Jamie Morgenstern, Briana Vecchione, Jennifer Wortman Vaughan, Hanna M. Wallach, Hal Daumé III, and Kate Crawford. Datasheets for datasets. In *Proc. of Workshop on Fairness, Accountability, and Transparency in Machine Learning*, 2018. 102

[85] Chaitanya Gokhale, Sanjib Das, AnHai Doan, Jeffrey F. Naughton, Narasimhan Rampalli, Jude W. Shavlik, and Xiaojin Zhu. Corleone: Hands-off crowdsourcing for entity matching. In *Proc. of SIGMOD*, pages 601–612, 2014. DOI: 10.1145/2588555.2588576 94

[86] Catherine Grady and Matthew Lease. Crowdsourcing document relevance assessment with mechanical turk. In *Proc. of MTurk@NAACL HLT*, pages 172–179, 2010. 89

[87] Mary L. Gray and Siddharth Suri. *Ghost Work: How to Stop Silicon Valley from Building a New Global Underclass*. Houghton Mifflin Harcourt Publishing, 2019. 14, 66, 72

[88] Mary L. Gray, Siddharth Suri, Syed Shoaib Ali, and Deepti Kulkarni. The crowd is a collaborative network. In *Proc. of CSCW*, pages 134–147, 2016. DOI: 10.1145/2818048.2819942 69

[89] David Alan Grier. *When Computers Were Human*. Princeton University Press, 2005. DOI: 10.1515/9781400849369 3

[90] Davide Grossi and Gabriella Pigozzi. *Judgment Aggregation: A Primer*. Synthesis Lectures on Artificial Intelligence and Machine Learning. Morgan & Claypool Publishers, 2014. 63

[91] Danna Gurari, Mehrnoosh Sameki, and Margrit Betke. Investigating the influence of data familiarity to improve the design of a crowdsourcing image annotation system. In *Proc. of HCOMP*, pages 59–68, 2016. 25

[92] Shuguang Han, Peng Dai, Praveen Paritosh, and David Huynh. Crowdsourcing human annotation on web page structure: Infrastructure design and behavior-based quality control. *ACM TIST*, 7(4):56:1–56:25, 2016. DOI: 10.1145/2870649 60, 96

[93] Derek L. Hansen, Patrick John Schone, Douglas Corey, Matthew Reid, and Jake Gehring. Quality control mechanisms for crowdsourcing: Peer review, arbitration, and expertise at family search indexing. In *Proc. of CSCW*, pages 649–660, 2013. DOI: 10.1145/2441776.2441848 57, 92

[94] Kotaro Hara, Abigail Adams, Kristy Milland, Saiph Savage, Chris Callison-Burch, and Jeffrey P. Bigham. A data-driven analysis of workers' earnings on Amazon mechanical turk. In *Proc. of CHI*, page 449, 2018. DOI: 10.1145/3173574.3174023 67

[95] Christopher G. Harris. Dirty deeds done dirt cheap: A darker side to crowdsourcing. In *Proc. of PASSAT*, pages 1314–1317, 2011. DOI: 10.1109/passat/socialcom.2011.89 72

[96] Kenji Hata, Ranjay Krishna, Fei-Fei Li, and Michael S. Bernstein. A glimpse far into the future: Understanding long-term crowd worker quality. In *Proc. of CSCW*, pages 889–901, 2017. DOI: 10.1145/2998181.2998248 63

[97] David J. Hauser and Norbert Schwarz. Attentive turkers: MTurk participants perform better on online attention checks than do subject pool participants. *Behavior Research Methods*, 48(1):400–407, March 2016. DOI: 10.3758/s13428-015-0578-z 55

[98] Chien-Ju Ho, Shahin Jabbari, and Jennifer Wortman Vaughan. Adaptive task assignment for crowdsourced classification. In *Proc. of ICML*, pages 534–542, 2013. 63

[99] Chien-Ju Ho, Aleksandrs Slivkins, Siddharth Suri, and Jennifer Wortman Vaughan. Incentivizing high quality crowdwork. In *Proc. of WWW*, pages 419–429, 2015. DOI: 10.1145/2904104.2904108 67

[100] Damon Horowitz and Sepandar D. Kamvar. The anatomy of a large-scale social search engine. In *Proc. of WWW*, pages 431–440, 2010. DOI: 10.1145/1772690.1772735 99

[101] John J. Horton, David G. Rand, and Richard J. Zeckhauser. The online laboratory: Conducting experiments in a real labor market. *SSRN eLibrary*, 2010. DOI: 10.3386/w15961 66

[102] Mehdi Hosseini, Ingemar Cox, Nataša Milić-Frayling, Gabriella Kazai, and Vishwa Vinay. On aggregating labels from multiple crowd workers to infer relevance of documents. In *Proc. of ECIR*, pages 182–194, 2012. DOI: 10.1007/978-3-642-28997-2_16 59, 89

[103] Jeff Howe. The rise of crowdsourcing. *Wired*, June 2006. 2

[104] Jeff Howe. *Crowdsourcing: Why the Power of the Crowd is Driving the Future of Business*. Crown Business, 2008. 2

[105] Gary Hsieh and Rafal Kocielnik. You get who you pay for: The impact of incentives on participation bias. In *Proc. of CSCW*, pages 821–833, 2016. DOI: 10.1145/2818048.2819936 63, 68

[106] Pei-Yun Hsueh, Prem Melville, and Vikas Sindhwani. Data quality from crowd-sourcing: A study of annotation selection criteria. In *Proc. of the NAACL HLT Workshop on Active Learning for Natural Language Processing*, pages 27–35, 2010. DOI: 10.3115/1564131.1564137 63

[107] Eric Huang, Haoqi Zhang, David C. Parkes, Krzysztof Z. Gajos, and Yiling Chen. Toward automatic task design: A progress report. In *Proc. of the ACM SIGKDD Workshop on Human Computation*, 2010. DOI: 10.1145/1837885.1837908 63

[108] Nguyen Quoc Viet Hung, Duong Chi Thang, Matthias Weidlich, and Karl Aberer. Minimizing efforts in validating crowd answers. In *Proc. of SIGMOD*, pages 999–1014, 2015. DOI: 10.1145/2723372.2723731 57

[109] Panagiotis G. Ipeirotis. Analyzing the Amazon mechanical turk marketplace. *XRDS*, 17:16–21, December 2010. DOI: 10.1145/1869086.1869094 66

[110] Panagiotis G. Ipeirotis. Demographics of Amazon mechanical turk. *Technical Report CeDER-10–01*, New York University, Stern School of Business, 2010. 66

[111] Panagiotis G. Ipeirotis and Praveen K. Paritosh. Managing crowdsourced human computation: A tutorial. In *Proc. of WWW*, pages 287–288, 2011. DOI: 10.1145/1963192.1963314 14

[112] Panagiotis G. Ipeirotis, Foster Provost, and Jing Wang. Quality management on Amazon mechanical turk. In *Proc. of the ACM SIGKDD Workshop on Human Computation*, pages 64–67, 2010. DOI: 10.1145/1837885.1837906 59

[113] Lilly Irani and M. Six Silberman. Turkopticon: Interrupting worker invisibility in Amazon mechanical turk. In *Proc. of CHI*, pages 611–620, 2013. DOI: 10.1145/2470654.2470742 69

[114] Lilly C. Irani and M. Six Silberman. Stories we tell about labor: Turkopticon and the trouble with "design". In *Proc. of CHI*, pages 4573–4586, 2016. DOI: 10.1145/2858036.2858592 72

[115] Ayush Jain, Akash Das Sarma, Aditya G. Parameswaran, and Jennifer Widom. Understanding workers, developing effective tasks, and enhancing marketplace dynamics: A study of a large crowdsourcing marketplace. *PVLDB*, 10(7):829–840, 2017. DOI: 10.14778/3067421.3067431 67

[116] Jin-Woo Jeong, Meredith Ringel Morris, Jaime Teevan, and Daniel J. Liebling. A crowd-powered socially embedded search engine. In *Proc. of ICWSM*, 2013. 99

[117] Ece Kamar, Severin Hacker, and Eric Horvitz. Combining human and machine intelligence in large-scale crowdsourcing. In *Proc. of AAMAS*, 2012. 63

[118] Ece Kamar and Eric Horvitz. Incentives for truthful reporting in crowdsourcing. In *International Conference on Autonomous Agents and Multiagent Systems, (AAMAS)*, (3 Volumes), pages 1329–1330, Valencia, Spain, June 4–8, 2012. 72

[119] Ece Kamar, Ashish Kapoor, and Eric Horvitz. Identifying and accounting for task-dependent bias in crowdsourcing. In *Proc. of HCOMP*, pages 92–101, 2015. 63

[120] Adam Kapelner and Dana Chandler. Preventing satisficing in online surveys: A "Kapcha" to ensure higher quality data. In *The World's 1st Conference on the Future of Distributed Work (CrowdConf2010)*, 2010. 55

[121] Toni Kaplan, Susumu Saito, Kotaro Hara, and Jeffrey P. Bigham. Striving to earn more: A survey of work strategies and tool use among crowd workers. In *Proc. of the HCOMP*, pages 70–78, 2018. 68

[122] David R. Karger, Sewoong Oh, and Devavrat Shah. Iterative learning for reliable crowdsourcing systems. In *Proc. of NIPS*, pages 1953–1961, 2011. 59

[123] Gjergji Kasneci, Jurgen Van Gael, David Stern, and Thore Graepel. CoBayes: Bayesian knowledge corroboration with assessors of unknown areas of expertise. In *Proc. of WSDM*, 2011. DOI: 10.1145/1935826.1935896 63

[124] Gabriella Kazai. In search of quality in crowdsourcing for search engine evaluation. In *Proc. of ECIR*, pages 165–176, 2011. DOI: 10.1007/978-3-642-20161-5_17 39, 41

[125] Gabriella Kazai, Jaap Kamps, Marijn Koolen, and Natasa Milic-Frayling. Crowdsourcing for book search evaluation: Impact of HIT design on comparative system ranking. In *Proc. of SIGIR*, pages 205–214, 2011. DOI: 10.1145/2009916.2009947 39

[126] Gabriella Kazai, Jaap Kamps, and Natasa Milic-Frayling. Worker types and personality traits in crowdsourcing relevance labels. In *Proc. of CIKM*, pages 1941–1944, 2011. DOI: 10.1145/2063576.2063860 39

[127] Gabriella Kazai, Jaap Kamps, and Natasa Milic-Frayling. The face of quality in crowdsourcing relevance labels: Demographics, personality and labeling accuracy. In *Proc. of CIKM*, 2012. DOI: 10.1145/2396761.2398697 90

[128] Gabriella Kazai, Jaap Kamps, and Natasa Milic-Frayling. An analysis of human factors and label accuracy in crowdsourcing relevance judgments. *Information Retrieval Journal*, 16:138–178, 2013. DOI: 10.1007/s10791-012-9205-0 89

[129] Gabriella Kazai, Natasa Milic-Frayling, and Jamie Costello. Towards methods for the collective gathering and quality control of relevance assessments. In *Proc. of SIGIR*, pages 452–459, 2009. DOI: 10.1145/1571941.1572019 90

[130] Gabriella Kazai and Imed Zitouni.   Quality management in crowdsourcing us-
      ing gold judges behavior.   In *Proc. of WSDM*, pages 267–276, 2016. DOI:
      10.1145/2835776.2835835 63

[131] Brian W. Kernighan and Rob Pike. *The Practice of Programming*. Addison-Wesley, 1999.
      74, 87

[132] Joy Kim, Sarah Sterman, Allegra Argent Beal Cohen, and Michael S. Bernstein. Me-
      chanical novel: Crowdsourcing complex work through reflection and revision. In *Proc. of
      CSCW*, pages 233–245, 2017. DOI: 10.1007/978-3-319-60967-6_5 100

[133] Kenneth A. Kinney, Scott B. Huffman, and Juting Zhai. How evaluator domain expertise
      affects search result relevance judgments. In *Proc. of CIKM*, pages 591–598, 2008. DOI:
      10.1145/1458082.1458160 25

[134] Aniket Kittur, Ed H. Chi, and Bongwon Suh. Crowdsourcing user studies with me-
      chanical turk. In *Proc. of CHI*, pages 453–456, 2008. DOI: 10.1145/1357054.1357127
      55

[135] Aniket Kittur, Jeffrey V. Nickerson, Michael S. Bernstein, Elizabeth Gerber, Aaron D.
      Shaw, John Zimmerman, Matt Lease, and John J. Horton. The future of crowd work. In
      Proc. of CSCW, pages 1301–1318, 2013. DOI: 10.1145/2441776.2441923 97

[136] Aniket Kittur, Boris Smus, Susheel Khamkar, and Robert E. Kraut.   Crowd-
      Forge: Crowdsourcing complex work. In *Proc. of UIST*, pages 43–52, 2011. DOI:
      10.1145/2047196.2047202 97

[137] Shailesh Kochhar, Stefano Mazzocchi, and Praveen Paritiosh. The anatomy of a
      large-scale human computation engine. In *Proc. of HCOMP Workshop*, 2010. DOI:
      10.1145/1837885.1837890 96

[138] Sarath Kumar Kondreddi, Peter Triantafillou, and Gerhard Weikum. Combining infor-
      mation extraction and human computing for crowdsourced knowledge acquisition. In
      Proc. of ICDE, pages 988–999, 2014. DOI: 10.1109/icde.2014.6816717 95

[139] Klaus Krippendorff. *Content Analysis*, 2nd ed., Sage Publications, 2004. 44

[140] Steve Krug. *Don't Make Me Think, Revisited: A Common Sense Approach to Web Usability*,
      3rd ed., New Rider, 2014. 36

[141] Pavel Kucherbaev, Florian Daniel, Stefano Tranquillini, and Maurizio Marchese.
      Crowdsourcing processes: A survey of approaches and opportunities. *IEEE Internet Com-
      puting*, 20(2):50–56, 2016. DOI: 10.1109/mic.2015.96 63

[142] Anand Pramod Kulkarni, Matthew Can, and Björn Hartmann. Collaboratively crowd-sourcing workflows with turkomatic. In *Proc. of CSCW*, pages 1003–1012, 2012. DOI: 10.1145/2145204.2145354 97, 100

[143] Abhimanu Kumar and Matthew Lease. Modeling annotator accuracies for supervised learning. In *Proc. of WSDM*, pages 19–22, 2011. 63

[144] Aditya Kurve, David J. Miller, and George Kesidis. Defeating tyranny of the masses in crowdsourcing: Accounting for low-skilled and adversarial workers. In *Proc. of GameSec*, pages 140–153, 2013. DOI: 10.1007/978-3-319-02786-9_9 63

[145] Dmitry Lagun and Eugene Agichtein. ViewSer: Enabling large-scale remote user studies of web search examination and interaction. In *Proc. of SIGIR*, pages 365–374, 2011. DOI: 10.1145/2009916.2009967 90

[146] J. Richard Landis and Gary G. Koch. The measurement of observer agreement for categorical data. *Biometrics*, 33(1):159–174, 1977. DOI: 10.2307/2529310 45, 46

[147] Walter S. Lasecki, Christopher D. Miller, and Jeffrey P. Bigham. Warping time for more effective real-time crowdsourcing. In *Proc. of CHI*, pages 2033–2036, 2013. DOI: 10.1145/2470654.2466269 101

[148] Walter S. Lasecki, Rachel Wesley, Jeffrey Nichols, Anand Kulkarni, James F. Allen, and Jeffrey P. Bigham. Chorus: A crowd-powered conversational assistant. In *Proc. of UIST*, pages 151–162, 2013. DOI: 10.1145/2501988.2502057 101

[149] Edith Law, Paul N. Bennett, and Eric Horvitz. The effects of choice in routing relevance judgments. In *Proc. of SIGIR*, pages 1127–1128, 2011. DOI: 10.1145/2009916.2010082 42

[150] Edith Law and Luis von Ahn. Input-agreement: A new mechanism for collecting data using human computation games. In *Proc. of CHI*, pages 1197–1206, 2009. DOI: 10.1145/1518701.1518881 100

[151] Edith Law and Luis von Ahn. *Human Computation*. Synthesis Lectures on Artificial Intelligence and Machine Learning. Morgan & Claypool Publishers, 2011. DOI: 10.2200/s00371ed1v01y201107aim013 3, 14

[152] Florian Laws, Christian Scheible, and Hinrich Schütze. Active learning with Amazon mechanical turk. In *Proc. of ACL*, pages 1546–1556, 2011. 63

[153] John Le, Andy Edmonds, Vaughn Hester, and Lukas Biewald. Ensuring quality in crowdsourced search relevance evaluation. In *Proc. of the SIGIR Workshop on crowdsourcing for search evaluation (CSE)*, pages 17–20, 2010. 56

[154] Matthew Lease. On quality control and machine learning in crowdsourcing. In *Proc. of HCOMP*, pages 97–102, 2011. 51

[155] Matthew Lease and Omar Alonso. Crowdsourcing for search evaluation and social-algorithmic search. In *Proc. of SIGIR*, page 1180, 2012. DOI: 10.1145/2348283.2348530 14

[156] Matthew Lease and Gabriella Kazai. Overview of the TREC 2011 crowdsourcing track. In *Proc. of TREC*, 2011. 89

[157] Hongwei Li, Bo Zhao, and Ariel Fuxman. The wisdom of minority: Discovering and targeting the right group of workers for crowdsourcing. In *Proc. of WWW*, pages 165–176, 2014. DOI: 10.1145/2566486.2568033 61

[158] Qi Li, Fenglong Ma, Jing Gao, Lu Su, and Christopher J. Quinn. Crowdsourcing high quality labels with a tight budget. In *Proc. of WSDM*, pages 237–246, 2016. DOI: 10.1145/2835776.2835797 63

[159] William Lidwell, Kritina Holden, and Jill Butler. *Universal Principles of Design*. Rockport Publishers, 2003. 36

[160] Bennet P. Lientz, E. Burton Swanson, and G. E. Tompkins. Characteristics of applications software maintenance. *Communications of the ACM*, 21(6):466–471, 1978. DOI: 10.1145/359511.359522 84

[161] Mark D. Lillibridge, Martin Abadi, Krishna Bharat, and Andrei Z. Broder. Method for selectively restricting access to computer systems—US6195698 B1. *USPTO*, 1998. 3

[162] Christopher H. Lin, Mausam, and Daniel S. Weld. Crowdsourcing control: Moving beyond multiple choice. In *Proc. of the 28th Conference on Uncertainty in Artificial Intelligence*, pages 491–500, 2012. 63

[163] Christopher H. Lin, Mausam, and Daniel S. Weld. To re(label), or not to re(label). In *Proc. of HCOMP*, 2014. 62

[164] Greg Little. Exploring iterative and parallel human computation processes. In *Proc. of CHI*, pages 4309–4314, 2010. DOI: 10.1145/1753846.1754145 101

[165] Greg Little, Lydia B. Chilton, Max Goldman, and Robert C. Miller. TurKit: Tools for iterative tasks on mechanical turk. In *Proc. of HCOMPWorkshop*, pages 29–30, 2009. DOI: 10.1145/1600150.1600159 91

[166] Greg Little, Lydia B. Chilton, Max Goldman, and Robert C. Miller. TurKit: Human computation algorithms on mechanical turk. In *Proc. of UIST*, pages 57–66, 2010. DOI: 10.1145/1866029.1866040 101

[167] Qiang Liu, Alexander T. Ihler, and Mark Steyvers. Scoring workers in crowdsourcing: How many control questions are enough? In *Proc. of NIPS*, pages 1914–1922, 2013. 63

[168] Sharon Lohr. *Sampling: Design and Analysis*. Brooks/Cole Publishing Company, Pacific Grove, CA, 1999. 78

[169] Eddy Maddalena, Stefano Mizzaro, Falk Scholer, and Andrew Turpin. On crowdsourcing relevance magnitudes for information retrieval evaluation. *ACM Transactions on Information Systems*, 35(3):19:1–19:32, 2017. DOI: 10.1145/3002172 90

[170] Andrew Mao, Ece Kamar, Yiling Chen, Eric Horvitz, Megan E. Schwamb, Chris J. Lintott, and Arfon M. Smith. Volunteering vs. work for pay: Incentives and tradeoffs in crowdsourcing. In *Proc. of HCOMP*, 2013. 68

[171] Adam Marcus and Aditya G. Parameswaran. Crowdsourced data management: Industry and academic perspectives. *Foundations and Trends in Databases*, 6(1–2):1–161, 2015. DOI: 10.1561/1900000044 14, 73, 81

[172] Adam Marcus, Eugene Wu, Samuel Madden, and Robert C. Miller. Crowdsourced databases: Query processing with people. In *Proc. of CIDR*, pages 211–214, 2011. 102

[173] Matthew Marge, Satanjeev Banerjee, and Alexander I. Rudnicky. Using the Amazon mechanical turk for transcription of spoken language. In *Proc. of ICASSP*, pages 5270–5273, 2010. DOI: 10.1109/icassp.2010.5494979 92

[174] Catherine C. Marshall and Frank M. Shipman III. The ownership and reuse of visual media. In *Proc. of JCDL*, pages 157–166, 2011. DOI: 10.1145/1998076.1998108 25

[175] Catherine C. Marshall and Frank M. Shipman III. Experiences surveying the crowd: Reflections on methods, participation, and reliability. In *Proc. of WebSci*, pages 234–243, 2013. DOI: 10.1145/2464464.2464485 68, 69

[176] David B. Martin, Benjamin V. Hanrahan, Jacki O'Neill, and Neha Gupta. Being a turker. In *Proc. of CSCW*, pages 224–235, 2014. DOI: 10.1145/2531602.2531663 69, 72

[177] Winter Mason and Siddharth Suri. Conducting behavioral research on Amazon's mechanical turk. *Behavior Research Methods*, 44(1):1–23, 2012. DOI: 10.3758/s13428-011-0124-6 87

[178] Winter Mason and Duncan J. Watts. Financial incentives and the "performance of crowds". In *Proc. of HCOMP Workshop*, pages 77–85, 2009. DOI: 10.1145/1600150.1600175 67, 68

[179] Steve McConnell. *Code Complete*, 2nd ed., Microsoft Press, 2004. 74, 87

[180] Richard McCreadie, Craig Macdonald, and Iadh Ounis. Identifying top news using crowdsourcing. *Information Retrieval*, 16(2):179–209, 2013. DOI: 10.1007/s10791-012-9186-z 87

[181] Tyler McDonnell, Matthew Lease, Mucahid Kutlu, and Tamer Elsayed. Why is that relevant? Collecting annotator rationales for relevance judgments. In *Proc. of HCOMP*, pages 139–148, 2016. 58

[182] Brian James McInnis, Dan Cosley, Chaebong Nam, and Gilly Leshed. Taking a HIT: Designing around rejection, mistrust, risk, and workers' experiences in Amazon mechanical turk. In *Proc. of CHI*, pages 2271–2282, 2016. DOI: 10.1145/2858036.2858539 24

[183] Robert C. Miller, Greg Little, Michael Bernstein, Jeffrey P. Bigham, Lydia B. Chilton, Max Goldman, John J. Horton, and Rajeev Nayak. Heads in the cloud. *XRDS*, 17, 2010. DOI: 10.1145/1869086.1869095 101

[184] Roozbeh Mottaghi, Sanja Fidler, Alan L. Yuille, Raquel Urtasun, and Devi Parikh. Human-machine CRFs for identifying bottlenecks in scene understanding. *IEEE Transactions on Pattern Analysis and Machine Intelligence*, 38(1):74–87, 2016. DOI: 10.1109/tpami.2015.2437377 90

[185] Barzan Mozafari, Purnamrita Sarkar, Michael J. Franklin, Michael I. Jordan, and Samuel Madden. Scaling up crowd-sourcing to very large datasets: A case for active learning. *PVLDB*, 8(2):125–136, 2014. DOI: 10.14778/2735471.2735474 63

[186] Andrew Ng. *Machine Learning Yearning*. mlyearning.org, 2019. 87

[187] Jakob Nielsen. *Usability Engineering*. Morgan Kaufmann, 1994. 36

[188] Scott Novotney and Chris Callison-Burch. Cheap, fast and good enough: Automatic speech recognition with non-expert transcription. In *Proc. of HLT-NAACL*, pages 207–215, 2010. 95

[189] Stefanie Nowak and Stefan Rüger. How reliable are annotations via crowdsourcing: A study about inter-annotator agreement for multi-label image annotation. In *Proc. of MIR*, pages 557–566, 2010. DOI: 10.1145/1743384.1743478 95

[190] Besmira Nushi, Omar Alonso, Martin Hentschel, and Vasileios Kandylas. CrowdSTAR: A social task routing framework for online communities. In *Proc. of ICWE*, pages 219–230, 2015. DOI: 10.1007/978-3-319-19890-3_15 100

[191] David Oleson, Alexander Sorokin, Greg P. Laughlin, Vaughn Hester, John Le, and Lukas Biewald. Programmatic gold: Targeted and scalable quality assurance in crowdsourcing. In *Human Computation*, 2011. 56

[192] Peter Organisciak, Jaime Teevan, Susan T. Dumais, Robert C. Miller, and Adam Tauman Kalai. Matching and grokking: Approaches to personalized crowdsourcing. In *Proc. of IJCAI*, pages 4296–4302, 2015. 61

[193] Peter Organisciak and Michael Twidale. Design facets of crowdsourcing. In *Proc. of iConference*, 2015. 63

[194] John Ousterhout. *A Philosophy of Software Design*. Yaknyam Press, 2018. 16, 87

[195] Patrick Pantel, Michael Gamon, Omar Alonso, and Kevin Haas. Social annotations: Utility and prediction modeling. In *Proc. of SIGIR*, pages 285–294, 2012. DOI: 10.1145/2348283.2348324 28

[196] Gabriele Paolacci, Jesse Chandler, and Panagiotis Ipeirotis. Running experiments on Amazon mechanical turk. *Judgment and Decision Making*, 5(5):411–419, 2010. 66

[197] Alexandra Papoutsaki, Hua Guo, Danae Metaxa-Kakavouli, Connor Gramazio, Jeff Rasley, Wenting Xie, Guan Wang, and Jeff Huang. Crowdsourcing from scratch: A pragmatic experiment in data collection by novice requesters. In *Proc. of HCOMP*, pages 140–149, 2015. 87

[198] Aditya G. Parameswaran, Hector Garcia-Molina, Hyunjung Park, Neoklis Polyzotis, Aditya Ramesh, and Jennifer Widom. CrowdScreen: Algorithms for filtering data with humans. In *Proc. of SIGMOD*, pages 361–372, 2012. DOI: 10.1145/2213836.2213878 60, 102

[199] Aditya G. Parameswaran and Neoklis Polyzotis. Answering queries using humans, algorithms and databases. In *Proc. of CIDR*, pages 160–166, 2011. 102

[200] Devi Parikh and C. Lawrence Zitnick. Human-debugging of machines. In *Proc. of NIPS WCSSWC Workshop*, 2011. 90

[201] Rebecca J. Passonneau and Bob Carpenter. The benefits of a model of annotation. *TACL*, 2:311–326, 2014. DOI: 10.1162/tacl_a_00185 45

[202] Ellie Pavlick, Matt Post, Ann Irvine, Dmitry Kachaev, and Chris Callison-Burch. The language demographics of Amazon mechanical turk. *TACL*, 2:79–92, 2014. DOI: 10.1162/tacl_a_00167 63, 67

[203] Eyal Peer, Laura Brandimarte, Sonam Samat, and Alessandro Acquisti. Beyond the turk: Alternative platforms for crowdsourcing behavioral research. *Journal of Experimental Social Psychology*, 70(Supplement C):153–163, 2017. DOI: 10.1016/j.jesp.2017.01.006 12

[204] Chenxi Qiu, Anna Cinzia Squicciarini, Barbara Carminati, James Caverlee, and Dev Rishi Khare. CrowdSelect: Increasing accuracy of crowdsourcing tasks through behavior prediction and user selection. In *Proc. of CIKM*, pages 539–548, 2016. DOI: 10.1145/2983323.2983830 61

[205] Alexander J. Quinn and Benjamin B. Bederson. Human computation: A survey and taxonomy of a growing field. In *Proc. of CHI*, pages 1403–1412, 2011. DOI: 10.1145/1978942.1979148 4

[206] Walter Rafelsberger and Arno Scharl. Games with a purpose for social networking platforms. In *Proc. of HT*, pages 193–198, 2009. DOI: 10.1145/1557914.1557948 100

[207] Vikas C. Raykar, Shipeng Yu, Linda H. Zhao, Anna K. Jerebko, Charles Florin, Gerardo Hermosillo Valadez, Luca Bogoni, and Linda Moy. Supervised learning from multiple experts: Whom to trust when everyone lies a bit. In *Proc. of ICML*, pages 889–896, 2009. DOI: 10.1145/1553374.1553488 59, 63

[208] Vikas C. Raykar, Shipeng Yu, Linda H. Zhao, Gerardo Hermosillo Valadez, Charles Florin, Luca Bogoni, and Linda Moy. Learning from crowds. *Journal of Machine Learning Research*, 11:1297–1322, 2010. 63

[209] Dennis Reidsma and Jean Carletta. Reliability measurement without limits. *Computational Linguistics*, 34(3):319–326, 2008. DOI: 10.1162/coli.2008.34.3.319 45

[210] Peter Robinson. Task complexity, task difficulty, and task production: Exploring interactions in a componential framework. *Applied Linguistics*, 22(1):27–57, 2001. DOI: 10.1093/applin/22.1.27 27

[211] Jakob Rogstadius, Vassilis Kostakos, Aniket Kittur, Boris Smus, Jim Laredo, and Maja Vukovic. An assessment of intrinsic and extrinsic motivation on task performance in crowdsourcing markets. In *Proc. of ICWSM*, 2011. 68

[212] Robert Rosenthal and Ralph Rosnow. *Essentials of Behavioral Research: Methods and Data Analysis*. McGraw-Hill, 1991. 36, 43, 51

[213] Joel Ross, Lilly Irani, M. Six Silberman, Andrew Zaldivar, and Bill Tomlinson. Who are the crowdworkers?: Shifting demographics in mechanical turk. In *Proc. of CHI EA*, pages 2863–2872, 2010. DOI: 10.1145/1753846.1753873 66

[214] Jeffrey M. Rzeszotarski and Aniket Kittur. Instrumenting the crowd: Using implicit behavioral measures to predict task performance. In *Proc. of UIST*, pages 13–22, 2011. DOI: 10.1145/2047196.2047199 60

[215] Marta Sabou, Kalina Bontcheva, Leon Derczynski, and Arno Scharl. Corpus annotation through crowdsourcing: Towards best practice guidelines. In *Proc. of LREC*, pages 859–866, 2014. 87

[216] Marta Sabou, Kalina Bontcheva, and Arno Scharl. Crowdsourcing research opportunities: Lessons from natural language processing. In *Proc. of I-KNOW*, page 17, 2012. DOI: 10.1145/2362456.2362479 87

[217] Gordon B. Schmidt. 50 days as MTurk worker: The social and motivational context for Amazon mechanical turk workers. *Industrial and Organizational Psychology: Perspectives on Science and Practice*, 8(2):165–171, 2015. DOI: 10.1017/iop.2015.20 69

[218] Falk Scholer, Andrew Turpin, and Mark Sanderson. Quantifying test collection quality based on the consistency of relevance judgments. In *Proc. of SIGIR*, pages 1063–1072, 2011. DOI: 10.1145/2009916.2010057 63

[219] D. Sculley, Gary Holt, Daniel Golovin, Eugene Davydov, Todd Phillips, Dietmar Ebner, Vinay Chaudhary, Michael Young, Jean-François Crespo, and Dan Dennison. Hidden technical debt in machine learning systems. In *Proc. of NIPS*, pages 2503–2511, 2015. 86

[220] Aaron D. Shaw, John J. Horton, and Daniel L. Chen. Designing incentives for inexpert human raters. In *Proc. of CSCW*, 2011. DOI: 10.2139/ssrn.1724518 39

[221] Victor S. Sheng, Foster Provost, and Panagiotis G. Ipeirotis. Get another label? Improving data quality and data mining using multiple, noisy labelers. In *Proc. of KDD*, pages 614–622, 2008. DOI: 10.1145/1401890.1401965 59

[222] Aashish Sheshadri and Matthew Lease. SQUARE: A benchmark for research on computing crowd consensus. In *Proc. of HCOMP*, 2013. 62

[223] Mark D. Smucker. Crowdsourcing with a crowd of one and other TREC crowdsourcing and web track experiments. In *Proc. of TREC*, 2011. 89

[224] Padhraic Smyth, Usama M. Fayyad, Michael C. Burl, Pietro Perona, and Pierre Baldi. Inferring ground truth from subjective labelling of venus images. In *Proc. of NIPS*, pages 1085–1092, 1994. 59

[225] Rion Snow, Brendan O'Connor, Daniel Jurafsky, and Andrew Y. Ng. Cheap and fast— but is it good?: Evaluating non-expert annotations for natural language tasks. In *Proc. of EMNLP*, pages 254–263, 2008. DOI: 10.3115/1613715.1613751 3

[226] Alexander Sorokin and David Forsyth. Utility data annotation via Amazon mechanical turk. In *IEEE Workshop on Internet Vision at CVPR*, 2008. DOI: 10.1109/cvprw.2008.4562953 3

[227] Paul Spector. *Summated Rating Scale Construction*. Sage Publications, 1992. DOI: 10.4135/9781412986038 36

[228] Jon Sprouse. A validation of Amazon mechanical turk for the collection of acceptability judgments in linguistic theory. *Behavioral Research*, 43:155–167, 2011. DOI: 10.3758/s13428-010-0039-7 63

[229] Chong Sun, Narasimhan Rampalli, Frank Yang, and AnHai Doan. Chimera: Large-scale classification using machine learning, rules, and crowdsourcing. *PVLDB*, 7(13):1529–1540, 2014. DOI: 10.14778/2733004.2733024 95, 96

[230] Siddharth Suri, Daniel G. Goldstein, and Winter A. Mason. Honesty in an online labor market. In *Human Computation*, 2011. 39

[231] James Surowiecki. *The Wisdom of Crowds*. Anchor Books, 2005. 2

[232] Charles A. Sutton, Timothy Hobson, James Geddes, and Rich Caruana. Data diff: Interpretable, executable summaries of changes in distributions for data wrangling. In *Proc. of the 24th ACM SIGKDD International Conference on Knowledge Discovery and Data Mining, (KDD)*, pages 2279–2288, London, UK, August 19–23, 2018. DOI: 10.1145/3219819.3220057 102

[233] Stefano Tranquillini, Florian Daniel, Pavel Kucherbaev, and Fabio Casati. Modeling, enacting, and integrating custom crowdsourcing processes. *TWEB*, 9(2):7:1–7:43, 2015. DOI: 10.1145/2746353 63

[234] Umair ul Hassan, Sean O'Riain, and Edward Curry. Effects of expertise assessments on the quality of task routing in human computation. In *Proc. of SoHuman*, 2013. DOI: 10.14236/ewic/sohuman2013.1 61

[235] Donna Vakharia and Matthew Lease. Beyond mechanical turk: An analysis of paid crowd work platforms. In *Proc. of iConference*, 2015. 12

[236] Jennifer Wortman Vaughan. Tutorial: Making better use of the crowd. In *Working Paper*, 2017. DOI: 10.18653/v1/p17-5006 14

[237] Luis von Ahn. Games with a purpose. *Computer*, 39:92–94, June 2006. DOI: 10.1109/mc.2006.196 4

[238] Luis von Ahn, Manuel Blum, Nicholas J. Hopper, and John Langford. CAPTCHA: Using hard AI problems for security. In *Proc. of EUROCRYPT*, pages 294–311, 2003. DOI: 10.1007/3-540-39200-9_18 2

[239] Luis von Ahn and Laura Dabbish. Labeling images with a computer game. In *Proc. of CHI*, pages 319–326, 2004. DOI: 10.1145/985692.985733 4

[240] Luis von Ahn and Laura Dabbish. Designing games with a purpose. *Communications of the ACM*, 51:58–67, August 2008. DOI: 10.1145/1378704.1378719 4

[241] Luis von Ahn, Benjamin Maurer, Colin McMillen, David Abraham, and Manuel Blum. reCAPTCHA: Human-based character recognition via web security measures. *Science*, 321:1465–8, September 2008. DOI: 10.1126/science.1160379 2

[242] Carl Vondrick, Donald J. Patterson, and Deva Ramanan. Efficiently scaling up crowdsourced video annotation—A set of best practices for high quality, economical video labeling. *International Journal of Computer Vision*, 101(1):184–204, 2013. DOI: 10.1007/s11263-012-0564-1 87

[243] Ellen Voorhees and Dona Harman. *TREC: Experiment and Evaluation in Information Retrieval*. The MIT Press, 2005. 29

[244] Jeroen Vuurens, Arjen P. De Vries, and Carsten Eickhoff. How much spam can you take? An analysis of crowdsourcing results to increase accuracy. In *Proc. of CIR Workshop*, pages 48–55, 2011. 63

[245] Aobo Wang, Vu Cong Duy Hoang, and Min-Yen Kan. Perspectives on crowdsourcing annotations for natural language processing. *Language Resources and Evaluation*, 47(1):9–31, 2013. DOI: 10.1007/s10579-012-9176-1 87

[246] Jiannan Wang, Tim Kraska, Michael J. Franklin, and Jianhua Feng. CrowdER: Crowdsourcing entity resolution. *PVLDB*, 5(11):1483–1494, 2012. DOI: 10.14778/2350229.2350263 94

[247] Jing Wang, Panagiotis G. Ipeirotis, and Foster Provost. Cost-effective quality assurance in crowd labeling. *Information Systems Research*, 28(1):137–158, 2017. DOI: 10.1287/isre.2016.0661 62

[248] Fabian L. Wauthier and Michael I. Jordan. Bayesian bias mitigation for crowdsourcing. In *Proc. of NIPS*, pages 1800–1808, 2011. 63

[249] Peter Welinder, Steve Branson, Serge Belongie, and Pietro Perona. The multidimensional wisdom of crowds. In J. Lafferty, C. K. I. Williams, J. Shawe-Taylor, R.S. Zemel, and A. Culotta, Eds., *Advances in Neural Information Processing Systems 23*, pages 2424–2432, 2010. 63

[250] Peter Welinder and Pietro Perona. Online crowdsourcing: Rating annotators and obtaining cost-effective labels. In *Proc. of CVPRW Workshop*, pages 25–32, 2010. DOI: 10.1109/cvprw.2010.5543189 63

[251] Jacob Whitehill, Paul Ruvolo, Tingfan Wu, Jacob Bergsma, and Javier R. Movellan. Whose vote should count more: Optimal integration of labels from labelers of unknown expertise. In *Proc. of NIPS*, pages 2035–2043, 2009. 59, 63

[252] Mark E. Whiting, Dilrukshi Gamage, Snehalkumar (Neil) S. Gaikwad, Aaron Gilbee, Shirish Goyal, Alipta Ballav, Dinesh Majeti, Nalin Chhibber, Angela Richmond-Fuller, Freddie Vargus, Tejas Seshadri Sarma, Varshine Chandrakanthan, Teogenes Moura, Mohamed Hashim Salih, Gabriel Bayomi Tinoco Kalejaiye, Adam Ginzberg, Catherine A. Mullings, Yoni Dayan, Kristy Milland, Henrique Orefice, Jeff Regino, Sayna Parsi, Kunz Mainali, Vibhor Sehgal, Sekandar Matin, Akshansh Sinha, Rajan Vaish, and Michael S. Bernstein. Crowd guilds: Worker-led reputation and feedback on crowdsourcing platforms. In *Proc. of CSCW*, pages 1902–1913, 2017. DOI: 10.1145/2998181.2998234 63

[253] Wesley Willett, Jeffrey Heer, and Maneesh Agrawala. Strategies for crowdsourcing social data analysis. In *Proc. of CHI*, pages 227–236, 2012. DOI: 10.1145/2207676.2207709 92

[254] Stephen Wolfson and Matthew Lease. Look before you leap: Legal pitfalls of crowdsourcing. In *Proc. of ASIS&T*, 2011. DOI: 10.1002/meet.2011.14504801135 71, 86

[255] Tingxin Yan, Vikas Kumar, and Deepak Ganesan. CrowdSearch: Exploiting crowds for accurate real-time image search on mobile phones. In *Proc. of MobiSys*, 2010. DOI: 10.1145/1814433.1814443 101

[256] Jie Yang, Judith Redi, Gianluca Demartini, and Alessandro Bozzon. Modeling task complexity in crowdsourcing. In *Proc. of HCOMP*, pages 249–258, 2016. 28

[257] Ming Yin, Mary L. Gray, Siddharth Suri, and Jennifer Wortman Vaughan. The communication network within the crowd. In *Proc. of WWW*, pages 1293–1303, 2016. DOI: 10.1145/2872427.2883036 69

[258] Omar Zaidan and Chris Callison-Burch. Crowdsourcing translation: Professional quality from non-professionals. In *Proc. of ACL*, pages 1220–1229, 2011. 57, 91

[259] Rabih Zbib, Erika Malchiodi, Jacob Devlin, David Stallard, Spyros Matsoukas, Richard M. Schwartz, John Makhoul, Omar Zaidan, and Chris Callison-Burch. Machine translation of Arabic dialects. In *Proc. of HLT-NAACL*, pages 49–59, 2012. 91

[260] Jing Zhang, Xindong Wu, and Victor S. Sheng. Learning from crowdsourced labeled data: A survey. *Artificial Intelligence Review*, 46(4):543–576, 2016. DOI: 10.1007/s10462-016-9491-9 62

[261] Dongqing Zhu and Ben Carterette. An analysis of assessor behavior in crowdsourced preference judgments. In *SIGIR Workshop on Crowdsourcing for Search Evaluation (CSE)*, pages 21–26, 2010. 39, 89

[262] Guido Zuccon, Teerapong Leelanupab, Stewart Whiting, Emine Yilmaz, Joemon Jose, and Leif Azzopardi. Crowdsourcing interactions—using crowdsourcing for evaluating interactive information retrieval systems. *Information Retrieval Journal*, 16(2):267–305, 2012. DOI: 10.1007/s10791-012-9206-z 89

Author's Biography

OMAR ALONSO

Omar Alonso is a Principal Data Scientist Lead at Microsoft in Silicon Valley where he works on the intersection of social media, information retrieval, knowledge graphs, and human computation. He holds a Ph.D. from the University of California at Davis and an undergraduate degree from UNICEN, Argentina.

Printed in the United States
by Baker & Taylor Publisher Services